First time knits

FUN PROJECTS TO TAKE YOU FROM BEGINNER TO KNITTER

LOUISE WALKER

PAVILION

First published in the United Kingdom in 2020 by
Collins & Brown
43 Great Ormond Street
London
WC1N 3HZ

An imprint of Pavilion Books Company Ltd

Distributed in the United States and Canada by
Sterling Publishing Co., Inc. 1166 Avenue of the Americas,
New York, NY 10036

ISBN 978-1-91116-362-6

A CIP catalogue record for this book is available from the
British Library.

10 9 8 7 6 5 4 3 2 1

Reproduction by Rival Colour Ltd, UK
Printed by Toppan Leefung Printing Ltd, China

www.pavilionbooks.com

Photography: Louise Walker
Graphic designer: Peter Butler

PUBLISHER'S NOTE: The author and publisher have made
every effort to ensure that all instructions in the book are
accurate and safe, and therefore cannot accept liability for
any resulting injury, damage or loss to persons or property,
however it may arise. It is the responsibility of the reader to
ensure that any toys, clothes or accessories made using these
patterns are safe for young children.

What's inside?

At 19 I discovered the world of knitting and it changed my life. I was a shy student studying commercial photography when I picked up my first pair of knitting needles. I'd seen a pattern for an English Breakfast Hat in a '70s *Jackie* magazine. I searched everywhere for a finished hat and, when I couldn't buy one, I asked my knitter Nan to make it. She didn't seem super keen. Her knitting specialism is making beautiful striped jumpers, which you'll often see me wearing.

Determined to have the hat, I learnt the basics from friends and family. I made my first knit with the help of my mum and sister one Christmas. It was a garish emerald green thing made of squeaky acrylic yarn. It was full of holes, really wonky and I absolutely loved it. I sewed it together badly and made it into a headband. I wore it to my bar job and the manager didn't seem super impressed by it.

After learning how to knit and purl I started on the hat and knitted the beret (plate), only to find I'd followed the vintage pattern completely wrong. I was so discouraged by my half disc of a hat, but didn't give up. I tried again, knitted the ingredients for the hat and was soon the girl who walked around Arts University Bournemouth in a retro breakfast hat.

Whilst at university I started incorporating my knits into my photography work. I'd knit all the time, even during lectures. When I graduated some of the images I made went viral and it gave me the opportunity to start my own business designing knitting patterns.

I've learnt so much on my knitting journey and I wanted to share my skills and love of the craft so that you can start your own projects. You may make mistakes along the way – I certainly did. Remember it's just yarn and you can always start again. Don't worry about getting egg on your face – wear it on a breakfast hat instead.

Meet me

Amala   Katie

This book will teach you how to knit over the course of nine projects. It's loosely based on how I taught myself. Starting with small and achievable makes, you'll progress up the craft ladder until you become a top knitter.

I've also invited four beginners to join you on your crafty journey. Over the last few months Amala, Katie, Simon and Zoë have been joining me at my Sheffield studio and I've been teaching them how to knit. They've learnt from scratch, using the same instructions and patterns as you.

and my knitters

Me   Simon   Zoë

Along the way, I've documented their progress and have included their common mistakes to help you identify any that you might make. There's also tutorials on how to fix them. I'm hoping that by finding and explaining the most common errors made by beginners, your learn-to-knit experience will be much smoother than mine. At the end of each project you'll also see their finished knits and reviews on how they felt about the process of making them.

Who are my knitters and why did they want to learn to knit?

Amala from Sheffield
I like making things, and I want to spend more time making things. I like all the possibilities, with colours and textures and sizes. I like to learn and learning something creative would be great.

Katie from Sheffield
I cross stitch and sew as a hobby and I love learning new creative things. My main inspiration for wanting to learn to knit was seeing Louise's patterns at a Christmas market. My dad loved the knitted Christmas pudding and I'd like to be able to make it for him as a gift.

Simon from St Albans
A good friend made me a beautiful scarf. I decided I wanted to do the same for others. The self-reliancy, creativity, therapeutic quality and achievement of completing items are also key reasons.

Zoë from Malta
I always wanted to learn how to knit because it was something my Nanna was really good at. She taught my mother how to knit, and my mother earned money from making jumpers when she was younger, so I always felt there was a strong family connection.

Where to start

At the beginning

As you turn the pages you're going to learn to knit. Unlike a lot of other instructional books I'm not going to give you pages and pages of technical information. Instead I've written this book like a course, where each project teaches you a new technique and builds on the previous skills you've learnt. There will be some technical information, plus handy downloadable extras from my website.

Each of the nine projects is colour coded. Important pages are earmarked with a little triangle in the corner, like this one here that says 'Hello'. There are different categories that you'll find in the corners. These are:

Project: These highlight the start of a new project.

Essentials: These pages contain technical information that relates to the projects or the knitting world.

Technique: What it says on the tin! These pages will teach knitting stitches and sewing techniques.

Pattern: These mark the start of a knitting pattern.

Sewing up: Most of the projects include sewing up photo tutorials.

Catch up: These pages feature the mistakes that my knitters made. You can use them to identity your own.

Fixing: If you've made a mistake and identified what it is, you can fix it using these tutorials.

Review: At the end of each project you'll find my knitters' reviews and photos of their finished knits.

Within each pattern you'll also find annotations written in green – these are helpful tips that will guide you through each project.

There's also the firsttimeknits.com website. You can use this as a hub when learning from this book. Every project has its own section with accompanying video tutorials for each technique. There are downloadable extras, like tick sheets, which you can use instead of writing in the book, design templates and colouring-in sheets to help customize some of the knits. You'll also find shopping lists, alternative yarn options and even bonus patterns.

Project 1:
Phone cosy
The absolute basics

My phone cosy is the perfect project to get you knitting. With this simple knit I'll teach you how to cast on, the knit stitch and casting off. It's knitted using super chunky yarn and big needles, so you'll be able to see what you're doing and it'll grow quite quickly. Before you know it you'll have made your first knitted item!

Materials

For this project the only things you'll need are a pair of 10mm (US 15) knitting needles, one ball of super chunky yarn and a darning needle. You can also use felt and some sewing supplies to decorate your cosy, but I'll tell you about that later.

Let's start with the yarn: super chunky yarn (also known as super bulky yarn) is the thickest type you'll find on the market. Yarn comes in different thicknesses that are referred to as weights, like in boxing. Using this analogy, super chunky would be the heavyweight of the knitting world. For this project, I'd recommend using a yarn that's made of acrylic as it's affordable and washes well. Pick a light colour as it will be much easier to see what you're doing when you're learning.

Next are your knitting needles: you'll need a pair of 10mm (US 15) straight needles. These are big needles to match the super chunky yarn. I suggest using a bamboo or wooden pair, but plastic is also fine.

Finally, you'll need a knitter's darning needle to sew up the project. As the yarn is super chunky it won't fit through a regular sewing needle, so you need to use a darning needle that has a larger eye. I prefer to use one made of plastic.

Your first task is to find the right yarn. I already mentioned that you'll need a super chunky yarn, but you have to find one with the same tension that I used for this project.

So, what does 'tension' mean? Tension (or gauge) is the number of stitches and rows you'll need to achieve when knitting a project to make sure that the

you'll need...

finished knit turns out correctly. You'll find the tension information on the paper band on the yarn – this is called a ball band. I'll explain more about tension later, as it's not super important for your first project. I just want to get you knitting!

The tension you need is: 8 stitches x 12 rows = 10cm (4in) on 10mm (US 15) needles. When searching for your yarn all you need to do is check the ball band (see example below). Ball bands come in different shapes and sizes but they all have the same information on them. It's always good to read the label, as knowing about your yarn is essential.

When you start knitting it's a great idea to head to your local yarn or hobby shop – they'll be able to help you find the right yarn and needles.

Alternatively you could buy your knitting materials online. On some websites you can even search for the tension you need! My top super chunky yarns for this project are: Plymouth Yarn Encore Mega, Scheepjes Roma Big and Patons Fab Big.

You can also find more yarn options, shopping lists, kits and materials at firsttimeknits.com.

Shade
Colour

Dye lot
261190

Country of origin

Brand
Name of yarn

100g, 50m/55yd

100% acrylic

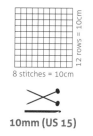

12 rows = 10cm

8 stitches = 10cm

10mm (US 15)

Brand: That's an easy one! There are lots of yarn brands to choose from.

Name of yarn: Yarns are given unique names and usually there is a clue to the weight of the yarn in the name.

Weight – 100g: This is where you need to know the difference between your yarn 'weight' and the actual weight of the ball itself. Super chunky is the 'weight' of the yarn, but the ball band will also include the actual weight of the yarn. Balls of yarn are usually sold in 50g, 100g or 200g balls.

Metreage (yardage) – 50m/55yd: The approximate total length of the yarn, which will be given in metres, yards or both. If you unravelled the ball and measured it you should have the amount stated.

Fibre – 100% acrylic: Details of what the yarn is made from. Yarns can be made from various different fibres, but I'll tell you more about that later.

Care instructions: How to wash your finished knit.

Tension – 8 stitches x 12 rows = 10cm (4in): That's what you're looking for! The band will usually include a grid and the number of stitches and rows that should be achieved when using the recommended needle size.

Needles or hook – 10mm (US 15): Ball bands will give you a recommended knitting needle or crochet hook size. This is the size needed to achieve the tension stated.

Country of origin: This is where the yarn has been produced.

Shade: Yarns come in an assortment of colours and often have shade names or numbers.

Dye lot: Each shade of yarn also has a dye lot. Yarns with the same dye lot number were dyed in the same batch. Make sure when buying several balls that they have the same number, or your project could change shade halfway through.

Slip knot

Not the heavy metal band

You've got your yarn and needles and you're ready to start knitting! If you were cheeky and skipped past the materials section, turn the page back, find out which yarn and needles you need and then we'll all be ready. Okay, now let's start knitting!

You're about to set sail on your knitting journey. Knitting and sailing don't have much in common but they do both use slip knots. A slip knot is a knot that creates an adjustable loop, so it's perfect for knitting. Before you actually get knitting you need to make

a slip knot. This slip knot will become the first loop on your needle. All the step-by-step tutorials in this book have accompanying videos on the firsttimeknits.com website. Simply find the project on the website, then find the technique and watch away.

1. Take approximately 60cm (24in) of yarn from the ball. You'll be using this to make your slip knot.

Tail

Yarn from the ball

2. Make a loop using the tail of the yarn. The tail needs to be underneath the loop.

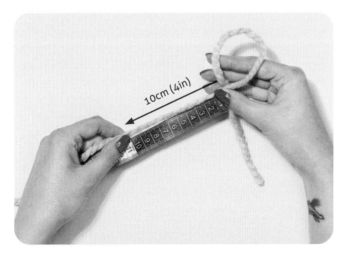

10cm (4in)

3. Pinch the loop using your right hand. Measure 10cm (4in) away from the loop towards the yarn coming from the ball.

First loop

Second loop

Yarn from the ball

Tail

4. After measuring 10cm (4in), make a second loop. The yarn coming from the ball should be on the top of this loop.

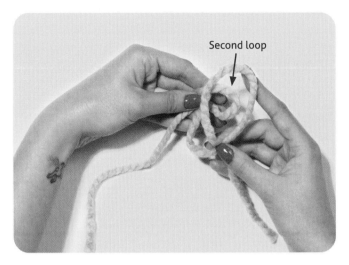

5. Still holding the first loop in your right hand, pinch the second loop with your left hand and thread it through the first loop from underneath.

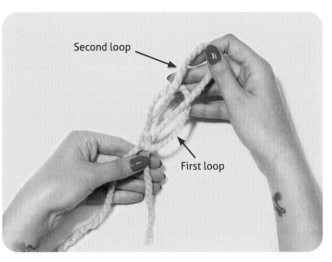

6. Grab the second loop with your right hand and pull it through the first one. Hold both tails of yarn with your left hand whilst doing so.

7. Still holding the second loop and the tails of the yarn, pull the second loop tightly, creating one new loop.

8. Adjust the new loop by pulling the yarn coming from the ball. Pull the yarn to make the loop smaller.

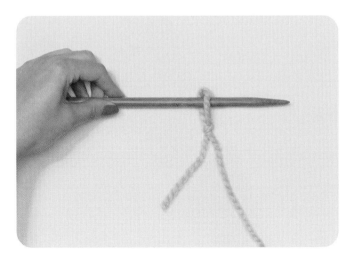

9. Take one of your knitting needles and place the loop you've just created onto it.

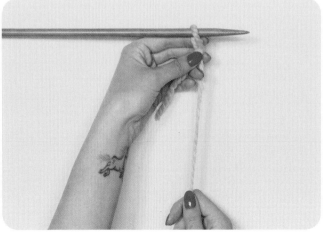

10. Pull the yarn coming from the ball until the loop is snug against the needle. You're now ready to cast on!

Casting on
Everything has to start somewhere

Casting on is the starting point for all projects. It's the first thing you'll be doing with the yarn and needles once you've made your slip knot. Casting on is the name for the technique that creates the first set of loops on the left needle. These loops will later become your first row of knitting. Here I'll be teaching you the two needle cast on method – it's a common casting on technique and is very similar to the knit stitch itself. Once you can cast on you'll definitely be able to knit. Follow these steps at your own pace and remember that you can always flick to page 15 to see how to avoid common mistakes. You can also watch my cast on video at firsttimeknits.com.

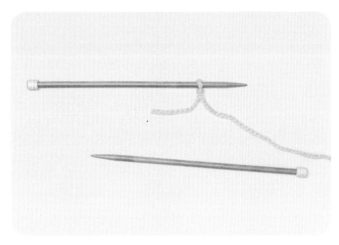

1. The loop made by the slip knot that has been placed on one of the needles is your first stitch. Place the needle with the stitch on in your left hand.

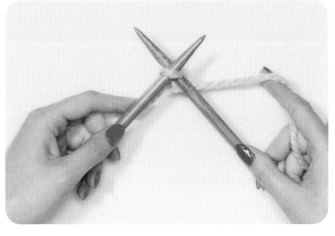

2. Using your right hand, place the other needle through the front of the stitch. Cross the needles as shown, with the right needle under the left needle.

3. Using your right hand, wrap the yarn from the back to the front of the tip of the right needle. Make sure that you use the yarn from the ball, not the tail from the slip knot.

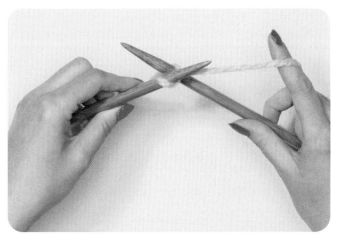

4. This is an aerial view of how the yarn will look once you've wrapped it around the right needle. Pull the wrapped yarn so it's not too loose or tight. It will sit between both needles.

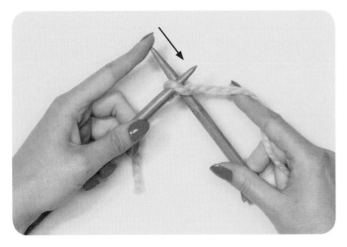

5. Holding the wrapped yarn and the needle in your right hand, use your left index finger to start pushing the right needle tip down.

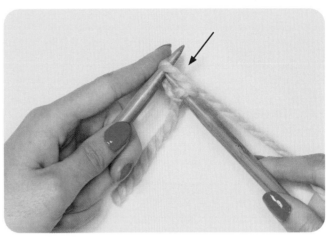

6. Continue pushing the right needle down and towards you so that it catches the wrapped yarn. The needles will now cross with the right in front of the left.

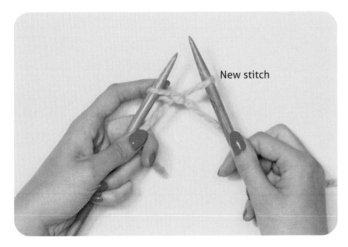

New stitch

7. After catching the yarn, pull the right needle away from the left, creating a new stitch on the right needle. The stitch you first pushed the needle through will be on the left needle.

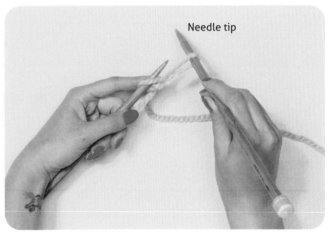

Needle tip

8. This is my favourite step. Twist the right needle tip down and away from you. This will twist the stitch. I always sing 'let's twist again' as I do it.

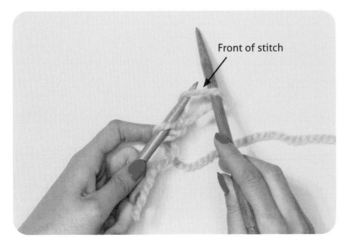

Front of stitch

9. With the right needle still in the twisted position, put the tip of the left needle into the front of the new stitch on the right needle.

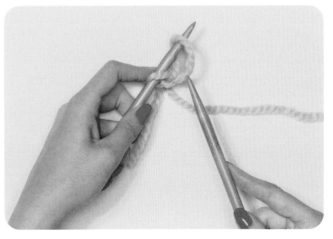

10. Once the new stitch is on the left needle, move the right needle away. Pull the yarn from the ball so that the stitch sits naturally on the needle. Don't pull it too tightly.

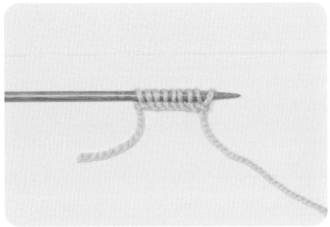

11. You've just cast on a new stitch! Repeat Steps 2–10 to cast on the next stitch. The newest cast on stitch will look slightly different to the others on the needle, but that's completely normal.

12. Cast on the number of stitches that the pattern specifies. These stitches can look squashed together, but don't worry – they'll spread out with the first row of knitting. For Project 1 see below for how many stitches you need to cast on.

Phone size templates

You've just learnt how to cast on (yippee!) and now you need the right number of stitches for the first project. All patterns will tell you how many stitches you'll need to cast on. For this pattern I've made it easy – simply place your phone sideways on the diagram below and cast on the number of stitches indicated in the box it fits into. If you feel like you need some more casting on practice, just continue casting on until you feel confident and then remove the additional stitches from the needle. This is done by sliding them off the left-hand needle. Once you've got the correct number of stitches on the left-hand needle, you'll be ready to start knitting.

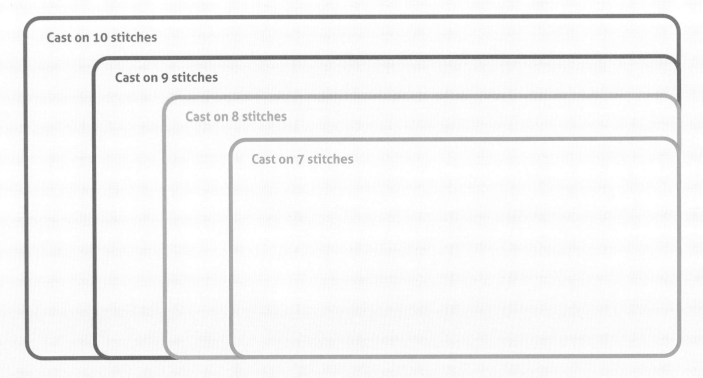

Cast on 10 stitches

Cast on 9 stitches

Cast on 8 stitches

Cast on 7 stitches

Cast on mistakes

A little bit of help

I've just finished teaching my knitters the two needle cast on method. It was our first meeting at the Sincerely Louise studio so everyone was getting to know each other. There was tea, crisps and, most importantly, yarn. Everyone chose a ball of super chunky yarn, made a slip knot, grabbed a pair of needles and started following the cast on steps. Along the way I answered their questions and helped when they needed me to. I also documented the mistakes they made. You can use these catch up pages to identify any mistakes you make and read tips on how to fix and avoid them. You will make mistakes when learning – that's completely normal and why I've included these pages! It's a great skill to realize when you've made a mistake so, when you do, these will offer a helping hand.

Simon made one of the most common mistakes – pushing the right needle tip into the front of the stitch by crossing the right needle over the top of the left. When knitting, always cross the right needle so that it's under the left, as shown in Step 2 of the casting on steps on page 12.

Here Katie pushed the needle into the back of the stitch. Although it doesn't look that different to Step 2, it's the wrong part of the stitch to push the needle through. The front of the stitch is the part of the loop that's closest to you, so when casting on push the needle through there.

I saw Zoë wrapping the yarn the wrong way around the needles, which would twist the cast on stitch. When casting on, wrap the yarn around the right needle from the back to the front and then in between the two needles.

When casting on don't forget my favourite step – the twist! This is important because if you don't twist it, the stitch will be facing the wrong way on the needle, like Amala's. If this happens take the stitch off the needle and cast it on again.

Knit stitch

It's finally knitting time

This is what knitting is all about – the knit stitch! The amazing thing about knitting is that you can make almost anything... like a cosy for your phone. For this project you're going to be knitting every stitch on every row and that's called garter stitch. This pattern creates a reversible corrugated fabric. When you knit you transfer the stitches from the left needle to the right needle, and it's as simple as that. There are two ways to do the knit stitch: the English or the continental method. These steps are for the English method but if you'd like to learn the continental version, head to page 19. If you're left-handed you may assume that you can't follow these instructions, but most left-handers find they have no problem with right-handed techniques. So what are you waiting for? Let's do this knit!

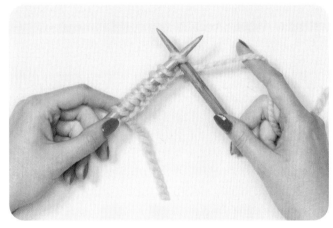

1. Knitting is similar to casting on. Just like when casting on, push the right needle through the front of the stitch to create a cross, with the right needle under the left.

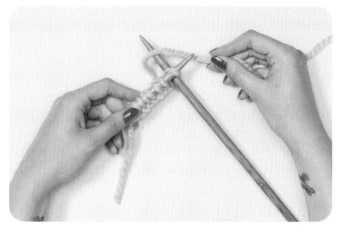

2. Again, like casting on, wrap the yarn from the back to the front of the right needle. Take the yarn with your right hand and pull it naturally, so it's not too tight or loose.

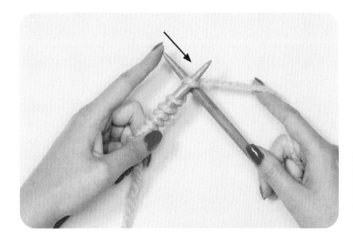

3. Use your left index finger to push the right needle down so that it begins to catch the yarn wrapped around it. Again, this is the same action as casting on.

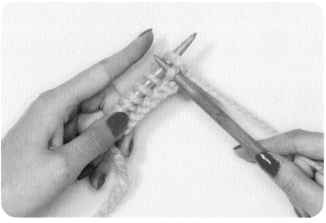

4. Catch the yarn, pushing the right needle down and out towards you so it crosses over the front of the left needle. This creates the start of a new stitch.

5. Now, unlike casting on, place your right index finger on the tip of the left needle and start sliding the stitch on the left needle up to your right index finger.

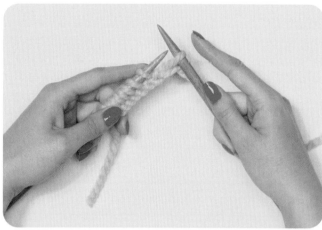

6. Remove your right finger and completely slide the stitch off the left needle. After knitting the first stitch you'll have transferred it from the left to the right needle.

7. With the new stitch on the right needle, repeat Steps 1–6 on the next stitch on the left needle. Repeat these steps for every stitch on the row, transferring the stitches from the left to the right needle, keeping the yarn behind the needles.

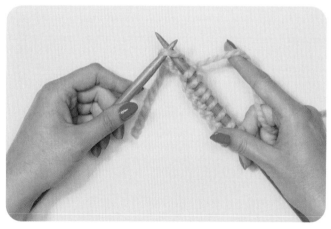

8. I'm always asked about the last stitch on the left needle. Just knit it exactly the same as the others! This will create a row of knit stitches. Check that you have the same number of stitches you cast on with. If you don't, go to page 21.

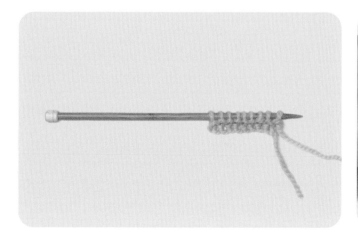

9. Once you've knitted the row you'll have created a set of bumps in the fabric. Turn the needle so it's facing the other way. The empty needle will now become your right needle.

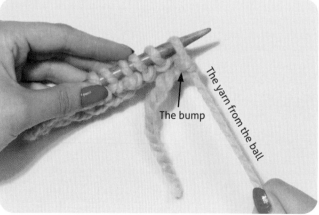

The yarn from the ball

The bump

10. At the start of the row, to tell which stitch to knit, pull the yarn tightly. The stitch being pulled, above the bump, is the one to knit. Push the needle through the front of that stitch.

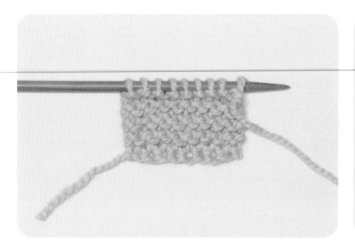

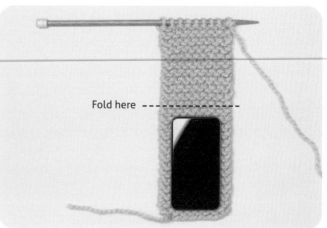

Fold here - - - - - - - - - - - - -

11. Continue knitting every stitch on the row, making sure you always knit above the bumps. Check your stitch count, turn the needle around and knit the next row. If you encounter any issues, head to page 21 for a bit of help.

12. Once you've knitted the number of rows specified in the pattern it's time to cast off. For the first project you need to knit a piece long enough to fold over your phone with an additional 2.5cm (1in).

How to read your knitting: garter stitch

So, you're knitting away and maybe you're thinking, what's actually going on? I wanted to get you knitting to show you just how easy it is, and now I think you're ready for some technical information.

The pattern you're making is called garter stitch. Garter stitch creates a reversible corrugated fabric that's stretchy. The edges won't curl so it's great for scarves.

As you knit you'll start to notice ridges forming in the fabric (see photo). Each ridge is made by knitting two rows.

To calculate the number of rows you've made, count the ridges and multiply them by two. I've knitted 13 ridges here, so I've worked 26 rows. If you can only see 12 ridges that's because I've counted the row on my knitting needle. You'll see that there's a ridge just under it – it's where you've been knitting above the bumps.

Remember to always include the stitches on the needle when counting your rows.

One ridge

Cast on edge – this is where you casted on

Cast on tail – when it's on the left side, the piece is facing the right way up

Continental knit stitch

Knitting European style

If you've just come from the English knit stitch page then welcome to knitting. What's great about knitting is that there are so many different choices, including how you make the knit stitch. This is the continental method. If you'd like to go back to the English method, you'll find it on page 16. With continental knitting you hold the yarn in your left hand, opposite the working needle. Some left-handers may find this more comfortable. As with the English method, the stitches transfer from the left to the right needle – it's as simple as that. If you've come from a later section in the book then that's fine too – you can use these instructions for any pattern that requires the knit stitch.

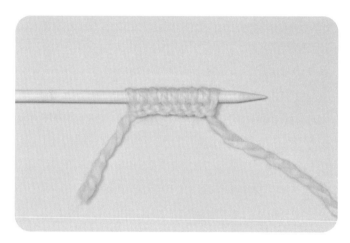

1. You've just cast on and this is how your stitches will look on the left needle. For now, hold this needle in your right hand with the needle tip facing to the left.

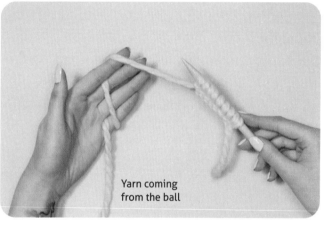

Yarn coming from the ball

2. Before you start knitting, move your left hand into the continental position. Wrap the yarn around your little finger, then up and around your index finger.

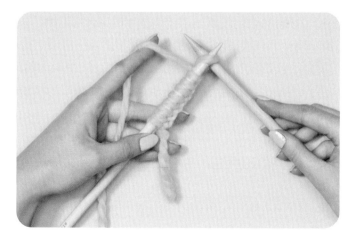

3. With your hand still in the continental position, move the needle with the cast on stitches to your left hand. Push the right needle through the first stitch, from the front to the back, just like when casting on.

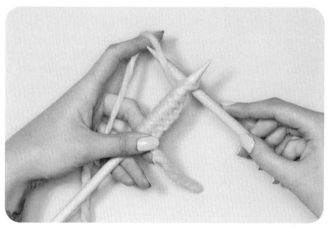

4. This is where knitting using the continental method differs from casting on and the English method. With your hand still in position, lay the yarn that you are holding with your left index finger over the right needle tip.

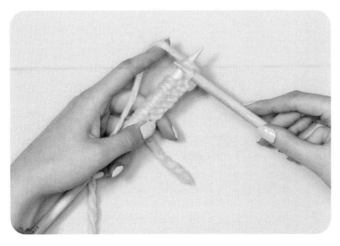

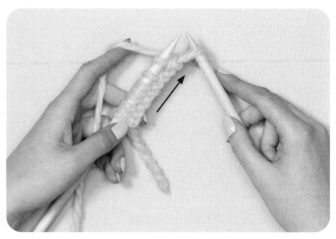

5. Catch the yarn using the right needle. This can be a little tricky at first. Then bring the yarn through the cast on stitch. Your left index finger can help when doing this.

6. Pull the right needle away from the left and slip the original stitch off the left needle. You can now see the new stitch on the right needle.

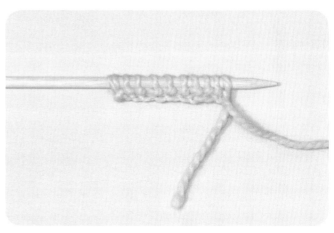

7. Repeat Steps 3–6 for every stitch on the row. Once you've knitted the row, check your stitch count to make sure it's the same number that you cast on with. If it's not, see page 21.

8. Turn the needle – it will now become your left needle and the empty one will become your right needle. The row that you've knitted has created bumps just under the needle.

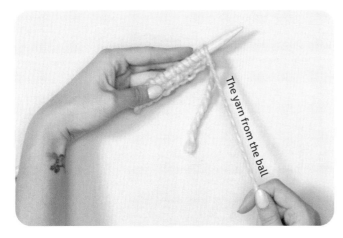

The yarn from the ball

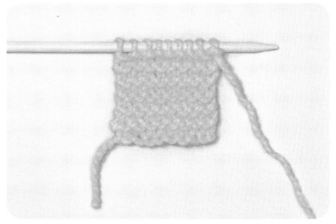

9. At the start of the row, if you can't tell which stitch to knit, pull the yarn tightly. The stitch being pulled, above the bump, is the one you need to knit. Move your hand back to the continental position and start knitting.

10. Continue knitting every stitch on the row, making sure that you always knit above the bumps. Check your stitch count, turn the needle around and knit the next row. For Project 1 see Step 12 on page 18 for your next instruction.

Knit mistakes

A helping hand when knitting

After casting on, I taught Amala, Katie, Simon and Zoë how to knit. They all learnt using the English method, but if you're a continental knitter these mistakes will still apply to you – you're just holding the yarn in a different way.

I always like to teach with super chunky yarn and big needles because you'll see what you're doing clearly, including any mistakes. On this and the next page I've included some of the common mistakes that my knitters made. Following this

are fixing pages, which show you how to correct some of these mistakes. They're also available as videos. If you've made a mistake not listed here you can head to the FAQ section at firsttimeknits.com for some extra help.

It can be tough to tell where the first stitch on the row is. Zoë pushed the needle into the stitch below the loop on the needle, which would add an extra stitch. Zoë's tip is to always pull the yarn to find the first stitch at the start of a row, which she's showing in the photo above.

Amala noticed an extra stitch at the beginning of the row. Like Zoë, she knitted into the wrong place. To fix this Amala needs to go back to the start of the row. See page 23 to find out how to unravel the work. Once you've unravelled the row, unravel the extra stitch and use Zoë's tip before starting.

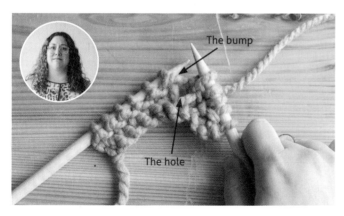

The bump

The hole

Here Katie accidentally knitted into the stitch below the bump. This not only creates a hole, it also adds an extra stitch. She'll need to unravel this stitch by pulling the right needle out of the stitch and pulling the yarn. To avoid this happening always knit into the loops above the bumps.

Simon has moved the yarn so that it's at the front of the work. When knitting, the yarn should always be at the back, behind the needles. If he was to wrap the yarn around the needle he would make a new stitch. He needs to move the yarn between the two needles so it's at the back of the work.

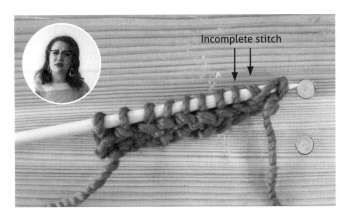

After turning the needle Zoë noticed she had an extra stitch. The stitch looked really strange, as if it was leaning to the right. This is an incomplete stitch from the row before, which means Zoë didn't finish the stitch whilst knitting it. The good news is that it's easily fixable! See page 24 for the tutorial.

As a new knitter it's really easy to drop a stitch. At some point all of my knitters dropped one and here's Amala's. To be honest even I still drop stitches! Don't panic – just head to page 25 to fix it. When dropping a knit stitch, a horizontal bar will appear in front of the dropped stitch.

It can be easy to get in a muddle when knitting for the first time, like Zoë has here. If this happens, pull muddled stitches off the needle and pull the yarn to unravel it back to one stitch. If the muddled stitch happened earlier in the row, then you'll need to go back to it by unravelling (see page 23).

This is something all knitters do, whether you're a beginner or have been knitting for years. Like Simon it's easy after the first row to knit with the cast on tail. You'll need to go back to the start of the row (see page 23) and use the yarn from the ball. You can trim your cast on tail to avoid this happening.

Katie asked why her yarn was over there? Your yarn should always be at the stitch you're about to knit. If it's not, you may have left it behind. Here Katie has slipped two stitches from the left to the right needle. To fix, just move the stitches after the yarn back to the other needle and then knit them.

Amala's top tip is to always check that you have the same number of stitches after each row. Keeping track of your stitch count after every row is great advice for any piece of knitting, especially when you're learning. If your knitting is looking uneven like Amala's, see page 26 for my tip.

going back in time

Unravelling your knitting at 88mph

Maybe you can't actually go back in time like in the *Back to the Future* films (the DeLorean had to reach 88mph, for those who didn't know!), but if you make a mistake you can go back and fix it. In this project I'm going to show you how to correct common issues. If you make a mistake, identify it and check these pages to see how to fix it. On this page I'll show you what to do if you realize you've made a mistake and have to go back to it. I like to call this 'going back in time' as it sounds much cuter than the real term of 'unravelling', especially as unravelling means undoing all your work. Unfortunately you can't jump back to where you started, but it's all good practice.

1. If your mistake happened on the row you've just worked, or on a row or two below, you can unravel the work stitch by stitch. Start by placing the tip of the left needle into the front of the stitch below the loop on the right needle.

2. Move the right needle completely away, letting the stitch on the right needle drop off. As you've already caught it with your left needle you won't lose the stitch, so you don't need to worry about dropping it.

3. Pull the yarn to unravel the stitch. Great Scott, you've just gone back in time!

4. Repeat this for every stitch you need to unravel until you reach the mistake, correct it and then start knitting again.

Incomplete stitches

Unfinished business

One thing I see happening a lot with beginners is incomplete stitches. Always check each row to make sure you haven't made a mistake. If you look at the row and notice that you have too many stitches it could be because you have an incomplete stitch. Incomplete stitches occur when you wrap the yarn around the needle but don't bring it through the stitch. An incomplete stitch will have the appearance of two stitches, and both will look slightly odd. If you were to knit both of them you'd accidentally add an extra stitch. You can either go back in time to where the incomplete stitch occurred or, if you can tell that you have an incomplete stitch, you can fix it by knitting up to it and following these steps. This saves time and you won't have to unravel and re-knit your work.

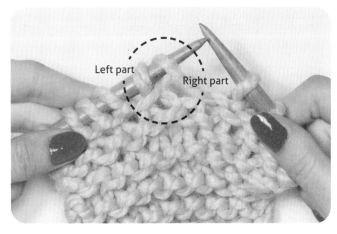

1. This incomplete stitch is in the middle of the row but they can happen anywhere. An incomplete stitch looks like two slightly odd stitches, with a left part and a right part (see photo). Knit up to the incomplete stitch.

2. Put the right needle tip through the back of the left part of the incomplete stitch. So far you've been knitting through the front of the stitches, so you'll need to do the opposite and put the needle through the back of this incomplete stitch.

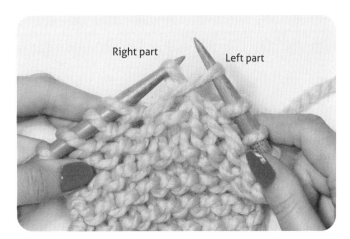

3. Use the right needle to transfer the left part of the incomplete stitch up and over the right part.

4. Remove the right needle. The incomplete stitch has been fixed and is ready to be knitted.

Dropped stitches

Pick them up

It doesn't matter if you're a beginner or an experienced knitter, it's really easy to drop a stitch. Dropped stitches occur when a stitch drops off your needle and then unravels. You'll see the dropped stitch and a horizontal strand running across it. When you drop a stitch you

need to pick it up straight away or, just like a pair of tights, it can unravel and ladder the work. A good tip is to have a safety pin attached to your knitting bag. Then if you drop a stitch you can quickly put it on the safety pin and that will stop it from laddering. If your stitch

does unravel and ladder down more than one row of your work, at this stage I would recommend unravelling to the dropped stitch and re-knitting. Or if this happens and you'd like to pick it up, refer to the advanced dropped stitch tutorial at firsttimeknits.com.

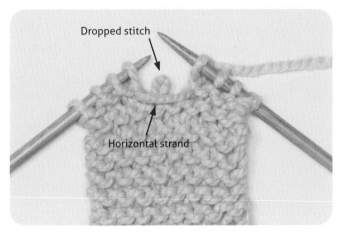

1. If a stitch drops off the needle, don't panic! If it hasn't unravelled, pop it back on the needle and knit it. If the stitch has dropped down a row, and unravelled with a horizontal strand running across the front of it, you'll need to pick it up.

2. Use the right needle tip to pick up the dropped stitch. Make sure you push the needle through the back of the dropped stitch – this is the opposite way to how you've been knitting so far, where you've been going through the front.

3. Put the right needle tip under the loose strand that's been sitting horizontally between the two stitches on the needle.

4. Using the tip of the left needle, pick up the dropped stitch and lift it over the strand.

5. You've just saved your stitch! But now it's on the right needle, which is the wrong needle as the stitch has not been knitted yet. You'll need to move it back to the left needle.

6. Transfer the stitch from the right to the left needle – this is called slipping a stitch as you don't need to knit it when moving it. Now the piece is ready to work as usual.

How to read your knitting: uneven stitches

If your knitting has too many or too few stitches and has wavy edges, then something is not quite right. My first piece of knitting looked just like this – it changed sizes throughout, but I still loved it. Your piece of knitting should be a straight rectangle, not like the piece shown here, which is a bit all over the place!

If your knitting is increasing in size and you have more stitches than you cast on with, this means you're accidentally adding extra stitches. You could be knitting under the bumps and then above them on the same stitch. This often happens at the beginning of a row. Or you may be knitting over both parts of an incomplete stitch, which would add an extra stitch.

If your knitting is getting smaller and you have fewer stitches on the needle than you started with, then you may have dropped a stitch, or you could have accidentally knitted two stitches together.

My top tip is to always check each row after you've finished knitting it. Look for any mistakes and fix them. You'll need to go back in time on the row (see page 23) to fix any issues, but it's better than having an uneven piece of knitting.

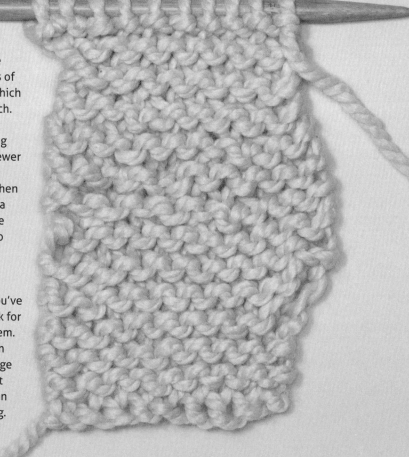

Casting off

Let's finish this knit

Once you've knitted all of the rows you need for your project it's time to cast off. This stops your knitting from unravelling. Casting off is also known as binding off or the finishing edge, but I'm going to refer to it as casting off throughout this book. Earlier,

I gave you two knit stitch options (the English method on page 16 or the continental method on page 19), but please note that most of the tutorials in this book are shown holding the yarn and needles in the English way. If you are a continental knitter, follow

the instructions but holding the yarn in your left hand in the continental position. My photos will look slightly different to your hands but will give the same results. Once you've cast off your first project you can officially say that you're a knitter. Welcome to the club!

1. Before you cast off, check that your cast on tail is on the left side of the work. If it's on the right, knit the row. Then knit the first two stitches on the next row as usual.

2. Take the left needle tip and push it through the front of the first stitch on the right needle. The left needle will cross over the right needle as shown.

3. With the left needle in the position, place your left index finger on the tip of the right needle.

4. Using the left needle, slide the first stitch up and over the second stitch and then up to your index finger.

5. Transfer the first stitch completely over the second stitch and off the right needle. The stitch that you cast off over will still be on the right needle – keep it there for now.

6. Knit the next stitch on the row as usual. Once again you'll now have two stitches on the right needle. Repeat Steps 2–5 to cast off the next stitch.

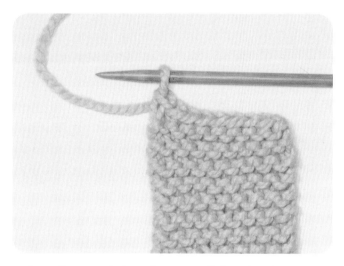

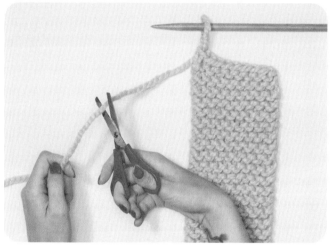

7. Cast off every stitch on the row until there is only one stitch remaining on the right needle.

8. Pull the stitch slightly so that it is looser on the needle. Cut the yarn, leaving a 60cm (24in) tail for sewing up.

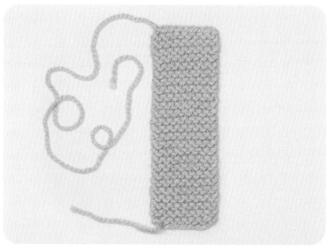

9. Carefully remove the stitch from the needle, thread the tail through the loop and pull tightly – this is the best bit!

10. That's it! You've just casted off and finished your knitting. Now it's time to sew it up.

Sewing up
Backstitch and weaving in

Most knitting projects require some sewing up. Throughout this book there are sewing up instructions for each project. As with the knitting tutorials I'll be teaching you sewing techniques and then referring back to them. Here I'm going to show you how to sew a basic backstitch to complete your phone cosy. Backstitch is a common seam used when sewing garter stitch pieces together. It can create a chunky seam inside the piece. I've used a contrasting coloured yarn here to demonstrate the process. When sewing up it's good to have some pins, a big safety pin or some spare yarn to hand to tack the pieces together. This will keep the work in place as you sew it up.

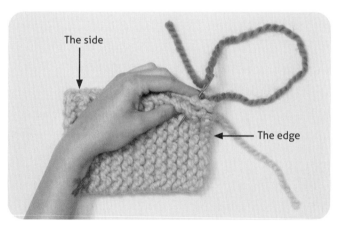

1. Fold the cosy in half so the cast on and off edges meet. Pin it together. Thread the cast off tail through a darning needle. From the back, push the needle through both pieces, 1cm (⅜in) from the side and 2cm (¾in) from the edge.

2. Pull the needle and yarn out of the work and move the needle back 2cm (¾in) to where the cast on and off edges meet. From the front, 1cm (⅜in) from the side, push it through both pieces of the knit. Pull it out on the other side.

3. Now push the needle and yarn 4cm (1⅝in) towards the fold, along the side of the work and through both pieces from the back. Then move it back 2cm (¾in) and sew into the piece from the front.

4. Continue the backstitch by measuring 4cm (1⅝in) along the back, coming through the piece to the front, measuring 2cm (¾in) back to where you've already sewn and sewing through the piece. Sew all along the side and cut the yarn.

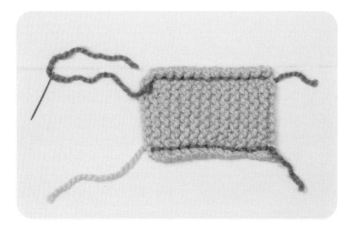

5. Repeat the backstitch on the other side of the piece. This time you won't have a tail to use. Cut a 60cm (24in) length of yarn and thread it through a needle. Starting at the open end, sew down to the fold, leaving a tail at the start of the work.

6. After sewing you'll have leftover tails. It can be tempting to cut these but they could unravel, so you need to weave them into the seams. Thread a tail through a darning needle, weave it into a few stitches along the seam, then trim.

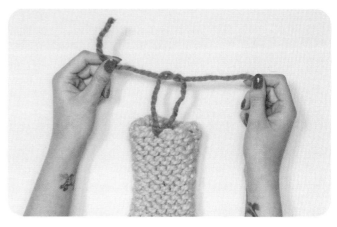

7. Weave the other three tails into the inside seams. Then turn the piece inside out. The backstitch will cause 1cm (⅜in) to be lost on either side of the cosy due to the seams, but this is normal when sewing up using this method.

8. To keep your phone from falling out of the cosy you can add a bow to the top. Cut a 60cm (24in) length of yarn and thread it through a darning needle. Sew through the centre on one side of the open edge and tie a knot.

9. Repeat for the other side of the cosy, cutting another 60cm (24in) length of yarn, sewing it through the centre and tying it in a knot. Trim the yarn if the lengths are different, so that all four pieces are the same length.

10. Tie the two sets of tails together in a bow. You can now decorate your cosy. You can download my template sheets, materials list and sewing techniques from my website, firsttimeknits.com, to customize yours.

Finished projects

How did they get on?

After each project I'm going to show you how my knitters got on. Throughout the book you'll be following their knitting journey. One of my favourite things about being a pattern designer is seeing your projects knitted in different colours, sizes and with unique personalisation. You can either follow my designs, customize yours using my knitters' ideas or come up with your own creations. Whatever you do I'd love to see photos of your finished knits! You can download templates to make the knitters' designs from the Project 1 section at firsttimeknits.com.

Amala: This was the first knit so I had to concentrate not to make mistakes. The mistakes were easy to spot though because the pattern was just knit, knit, knit. It was a really good project to learn and at the end of it I had a finished phone cosy. I loved that I could make mine into whatever I wanted and I chose a cartoon horse.

Katie: I loved making the phone cosy. I enjoyed how chunky it was as I could easily see my mistakes. It was quicker to knit than I thought, as we all knitted and decorated them in just an afternoon. The yarn is one of my favourite colours and I customized the cosy with mini pompoms as I thought they were really cute.

Simon: This was a nice introduction to the knit stitch and backstitch sewing technique. I absolutely loved working with the super chunky yarn and big needles and how quickly I knitted the cosy. I made an orangutan because they're part of the great ape family and therefore one of my favourite animals.

Zoë: I loved this project! It really tested my skills in terms of mastering the cast on and the knit stitch, and it was so easy to put together. It definitely gave me the confidence I needed to start my knitting journey. I chose blue yarn because I was immediately drawn to how much it looked like the colour of the sea in Malta!

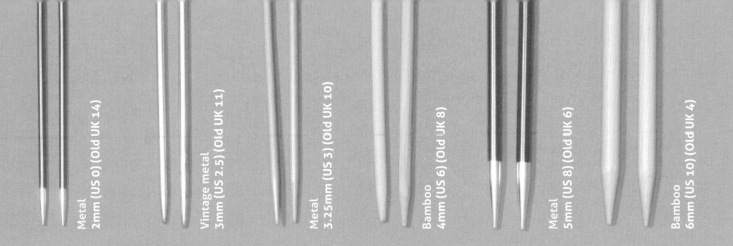

Metal
2mm (US 0) (Old UK 14)

Vintage metal
3mm (US 2.5) (Old UK 11)

Metal
3.25mm (US 3) (Old UK 10)

Bamboo
4mm (US 6) (Old UK 8)

Metal
5mm (US 8) (Old UK 6)

Bamboo
6mm (US 10) (Old UK 4)

Needles and yarn

Now you're officially a knitter I can tell you more about needles and yarn. Your first project was knitted using big needles and super chunky yarn, but there's a huge range of yarns with accompanying needle sizes.

Along the top of the page you'll see a range of knitting needles. Different needle sizes are needed for different weights of yarn. On a yarn's ball band a needle size will be suggested, so it's easy to find what you need. The above needles correspond to the below yarns to give you an idea of which size you should use with each weight of yarn.

Each thickness of needle has its own size name. There are three ways in

which knitting needles can be named: in metric, US or in old UK and Canadian sizes. For example the first needle on the left of this page is 2mm in the metric size – this refers to the diameter of the needle. In US sizes it's known as a size 0. US sizes start with low numbers for small needles, with the number rising for larger diameter needles. This size is known as a size 14 in old UK sizes (which are also Canadian sizes) – this naming system is opposite to US needles, with the high numbers referring to smaller diameters and decreasing for the larger ones.

I've included the metric and US sizes in my patterns – the metric size will come first with the US size in brackets. Old

UK sizes are mainly found in vintage patterns and you may stumble across a fancy-looking pair in a charity shop. They're fine to use as long as you know what size they're equivalent to.

You'll also find metric needles in half or quarter sizes, like 3.25mm (US 3) needles. You'll find the size written on the knitting needle, usually on the side or the top. A needle size gauge is a handy tool to have – there's one in the top right corner on the next page. If you're unsure which size your needle is, you can poke it through the holes and see which one it fits into. Throughout this book you'll mainly be using big needles, but you can find a conversion chart for all sizes at firsttimeknits.com.

0: Lace, 4-ply, 10-count, fingering
1.5mm–2.25mm (US 000–1)

1: Super fine, 4-ply, sock, baby
2.25mm–3.25mm (US 1–3)

2: Fine, lightweight DK, baby, sport
3.25–3.75mm (US 3–5)

3: Light DK, lightweight, worsted
3.75mm–4.5mm (US 5–7)

4: Medium aran, worsted, afghan
4.5mm–5.5mm (US 7–9)

5: Bulky, chunky, craft, rug
5.5mm–8mm (US 9–11)

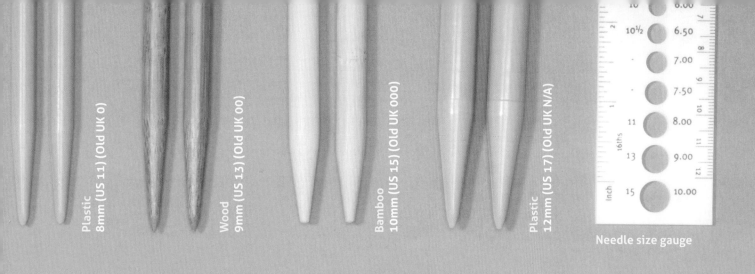

Plastic
8mm (US 11) (Old UK 0)

Wood
9mm (US 13) (Old UK 00)

Bamboo
10mm (US 15) (Old UK 000)

Plastic
12mm (US 17) (Old UK N/A)

Needle size gauge

Like yarn, needles are made using different materials and I've listed each material above the size. I recommend bamboo for beginners as the stitches won't slip on the needles. Thinner needles tend to be made from metal, as wood or bamboo would easily snap, and larger needles are usually made from bamboo or plastic. You may prefer to buy a set of needles as you'll be using a range of sizes, or you could get them project by project and try different materials – you'll soon find that you have a favourite.

Along the bottom of the page are different weights of yarn. I'll tell you about their fibre content later. The weight of the yarn refers to its thickness and is not to be confused with the actual weight of the ball. Directly beneath each needle size is the weight of yarn you'd typically knit with. Yarn weights have different

names and categories – these are numbered, from low to high, reflecting the weight of the yarn.

The thinnest yarn weight is known as lace – these are the really thin yarns and are often used for, you guessed it, lacy knits! These knits are beautiful and intricate. Then there's super fine and fine, which are great for shawls and socks. Following these are the lightweight and DK sizes, with DK being short for 'double knit'. These are pretty standard weights and you'll find lots of things are knitted in DK, from toys to garments. The next thickness is aran, which was historically used to make the classic fishermen's jumpers.

Then there's chunky yarn, which is one of my favourites. This is a slightly broader category as you can knit these yarns on a wider range of needle sizes. This also applies to super chunky and

jumbo yarns and that's why I had to be specific with which yarn you needed for your first knit! The chunkier the yarn the quicker it knits up.

I've included some other handy tools here, like point protectors. You put these at the end of your needles when you're not knitting to stop the work from falling off. Crochet hooks are good to have on hand as you can use them for picking up dropped stitches following my online tutorial. Row counters are also great when working from patterns – I've included some information about them on page 36.

Over the next eight projects I'm going to introduce you to a range of yarn weights and needle sizes. The next project is made using chunky yarn.

5: Bulky, chunky, craft, rug
5.5mm–8mm (US 9–11)

6: Super bulky, super chunky, bulky, roving
8mm–12.75mm (US 11–17)

6: Super bulky, super chunky, bulky, roving
8mm–12.75mm (US 11–17)

7: Jumbo
12.75mm and larger (US 17 and larger)

Crochet hook

Row counters

Point protectors

Project 2:
Cup warmer

Pattern reading and increasing

My cup warmer builds on the skills that you learnt in Project 1, but this time you'll be working from a pattern. I often hear people say they can knit but can't follow a pattern, so rather than putting it off you're going to learn that now! There are three variations of this pattern – I've made a bear but you can see my knitters' designs on page 44.

Pattern reading

It's like crafty coding

What is a knitting pattern? Where do you start with it? What does it all mean? Well, the good news is that you're about to find out. Patterns are very much like recipes – you've got your ingredients (the yarn and needles) and some instructions. Now you know how to knit, you just need to know how to read the codes that make up patterns. I've deconstructed my knitting pattern to help you get started. This is a basic pattern and it includes a couple of new techniques. I've added annotations in **green** to explain everything. These wouldn't be on a regular pattern but will appear throughout this book. Start by reading the introduction – you'll find your first task for this project in there.

How to read a pattern

SKILL LEVEL
Patterns will tell you the skill level needed. I've included these in circles at the top of each pattern.

MATERIALS
Stylecraft Special Chunky yarn
(chunky, 100% acrylic, 144m per 100g):
Here you'll find the yarn recommended by the designer. It'll include the basic information from the ball band, like the name, weight, fibre type and metreage.

M (main colour) – Gold, 1 ball
C (contrast colour) – Black, tiny amount
Some patterns require more than one colour of yarn. M (or MC) refers to the main colour and C (or CC) refers to a contrast colour. Some patterns may ask for more colours and label them in a different way, such as A, B, C, D, etc. I've chosen gold for my cup warmer but you can pick whatever you'd like for the main colour – see my knitters' reviews on page 44 for some inspiration.

6mm (US 10) needles
The pattern will also tell you what size needles you need. The needle sizes may be listed in metric (mm), US or even old UK and Canadian sizes. This pattern asks for 6mm (US 10) needles, but you should also have 5mm and 7mm (US 8 and 10½) needles. I'll explain why very soon.

Darning needle and row counter
You may also need some additional materials. Here you need a darning needle and a row counter (see page 36 for more information on those).

TENSION
14 stitches x 26 rows = 10cm (4in) in garter stitch on 6mm (US 10) needles
Tension (or gauge) is one of the most important things in knitting and your first task will be to make a tension square.

When choosing your yarn you'll find that the recommended yarn suggests a tension of 14 stitches x 20 rows. Don't worry that this is different to what is listed in the pattern. Just make sure that the yarn you use has a 14-stitch tension written on the ball band – the number of rows shown on the ball band will be different to the 26 asked for here.

ABBREVIATIONS
K Knit
Kfb Knit into the front and back of the same stitch (increase)
... Repeat the instructions within the asterisks
(sts) Stitches: This refers to the number of stitches you'll have at the end of a row after increasing or decreasing
These are the abbreviations featured in the pattern. Abbreviations are used to save space and really are just like a code. This pattern uses K (the knit stitch) and Kfb (which is the new stitch you're going to learn), as well as *...* (which means that parts of the pattern will be repeated).

FINISHED SIZE: Fits a small or medium reusable coffee cup
All patterns will include the finished size of the knitted piece. This project only comes in one size, but other patterns, like garments, offer different sizes.

Once you've read through this page and have your yarn and needles ready, head to the next page.

Knitting tips
Holding the yarn and counting rows

Your first task of Project 2 is to make a tension square. Before you do this I want to give you a couple of tips. These will help when knitting your square as well as for future projects. The first tip is about knitting using the English method. As a beginner you've been getting to grips with the knit stitch. With the English method the first thing that lots of books will tell you is how to hold the yarn properly. I didn't tell you about that earlier as I think it's more important to get the knit stitch right. Holding the yarn in the right way regulates how tight or loose the yarn coming from the ball is. If you're a continental knitter then you can ignore my first two tips and go straight to tip 3 which is all about row counting. You're going to be knitting lots of rows again and will need to count them.

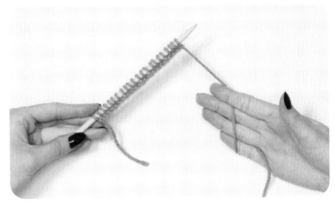

1. To help with your tension when knitting using the English method wrap the yarn from the ball around your little finger, then up and between your index and second fingers. The yarn will run over your index finger when knitting.

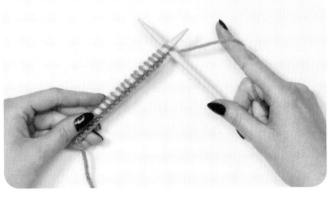

2. Grab the other needle in your right hand. Place your hands over the top of both needles to hold them. Use your thumb and finger to support them. Place your hands near the tips of the needles, but not right at the end of them.

3. This is a row counter – it's a little plastic thing that keeps track of your rows. They come in different sizes, so if you're going to use one make sure it's the right one for your needles, which are 6mm (US 10) for this project.

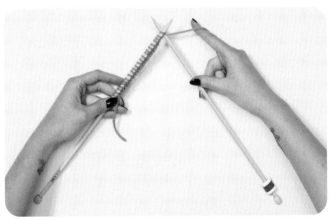

4. Once you've cast on, slide the row counter up the empty needle and move the numbers every time you finish a row. There are also row counter apps available. You don't have to use a counter – you can check by reading the knitting instead.

Tension

No need to stress!

Here's your first task of Project 2. You will need a tape measure, your yarn (I recommend Stylecraft Special Chunky yarn) and needles in the following sizes: 5mm, 6mm, 7mm (US 8, 10, 10½).

Checking your tension is the first thing you should do before starting a project. It's easy to overlook, but it is essential.

You can check your tension by making a square – this is called a swatch. Patterns will always recommend a tension (or gauge), which is the number of stitches and rows you need to achieve when making your square. Getting your tension right is really important when making garments or things that need to fit, like this cup warmer.

Before making your cup warmer you need to check your tension. My pattern

is asking for a tension of 14 stitches x 26 rows in garter stitch on 6mm (US 10) needles = 10cm (4in). This means that if you knit 14 stitches and 26 rows using 6mm (US 10) needles you should make a 10cm x 10cm (4in x 4in) square. Before you get started it's a good rule of thumb to cast on 4 more stitches than asked for and work 4 extra rows. Cast on 18 stitches and knit 30 rows using 6mm (US 10) needles and the recommended yarn to make your tension square.

Once you've cast off, place your cast on and cast off tails to the left of the work – this will mean that the 'right side' is facing you. Grab a tape measure and lay it horizontally with the end one or two stitches in from the side. Measure 10cm (4in) and count the stitches within the 0–10cm (0–4in) area – you should have 14. Lay the tape measure vertically one

ridge below the cast off edge. Count the rows within the 0–10cm (0–4in) area – you should have 13 ridges, which is 26 rows. If you do, you're ready to start knitting. If it's bigger or smaller than that, you'll need to adjust your tension. It is difficult to change the way you knit so you can change your needle size.

If you have too many stitches and rows within the 10cm (4in) area, make another swatch using the 5mm (US 8) needles and measure. If you don't have enough stitches or rows within the 10cm (4in) area, make another swatch using the 7mm (US 10½) needles and measure.

It's totally normal to have to change your tension. Once you have the right tension you can start knitting the project using your chosen needles.

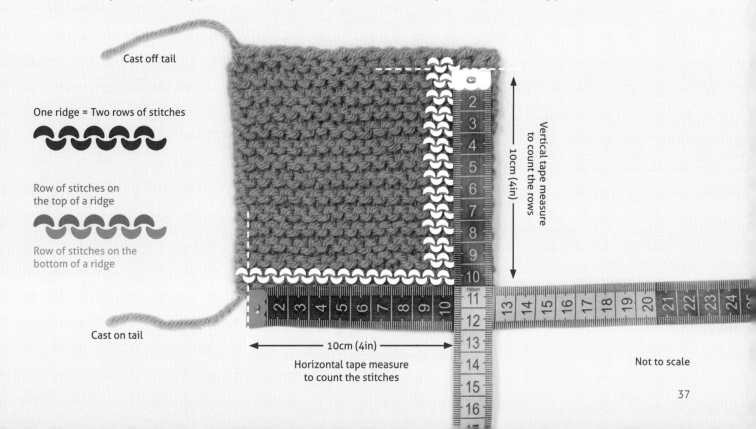

Cast off tail

One ridge = Two rows of stitches

Row of stitches on the top of a ridge

Row of stitches on the bottom of a ridge

Cast on tail

Vertical tape measure to count the rows

10cm (4in)

10cm (4in)

Horizontal tape measure to count the stitches

Not to scale

Cup warmer

MATERIALS

Stylecraft Special Chunky yarn (chunky, 100% acrylic, 144m per 100g):
M (main colour) – Gold, 1 ball
C (contrast colour) – Black, tiny amount

6mm (US 10) needles

Darning needle and row counter

TENSION

14 stitches x 26 rows = 10cm (4in) in garter stitch on 6mm (US 10) needles

ABBREVIATIONS

K Knit
Kfb Knit into the front and back of the same stitch (increase)
... Repeat the instructions within the asterisks
(sts) Stitches: This refers to the number of stitches you'll have at the end of a row after increasing or decreasing

FINISHED SIZE: Fits a small or medium reusable coffee cup

Once you've looked at the materials section and have made your swatch it's time to start knitting. Patterns can seem really daunting at first, but they're just a set of instructions that turn yarn into something cute. You'll find that most patterns are written in columns – this is to save space.

I've deconstructed this pattern, explaining each part for you. All the instructions to help you are shown in green. I've also included a new stitch technique, so keep an eye out for that!

There are different variations for this pattern. You can make a bear, fox, cat or rabbit. All of the variations use the same basic cup warmer pattern.

CUP WARMER – make one
Patterns will tell you which part of the project you're making. Here we're knitting the cup warmer piece. 'Make one' refers to the number of pieces you need to knit. Here you need to make one cup warmer piece.

Cast on 30 stitches in M using 6mm (US 10) needles.
Hey, remember that cast on thing you did back on page 12? Well you're doing it all over again. Every project starts by casting on. Here you need to cast on 30 stitches in M. As I mentioned in the materials section, M is the main colour that you've chosen for your cup warmer. The pattern also mentions the needle size, but if you swatched and

found you achieved the right tension on a different size, use those instead.

Row 1 K
Each row represents a step in the pattern and includes the instructions needed for that line of stitches. When you made the phone cosy you knitted lots of rows!

Here, Row 1 asks you to K. Looking at our abbreviations in the introduction above, K means knit, so you need to knit every stitch on the row. Once you've finished knitting the row check that you have the same number of stitches you cast on – that's 30.

Row 2 K
Your second row is also asking you to K, so knit every stitch.

Row 3 *Kfb, K9* three times (33 sts)
The third row is where all the fun is going to happen. Row 3 introduces the new technique, Kfb (knitting into the front and the back of the same stitch). See page 40 for the Kfb tutorial and apply it to the first stitch of this row. Then return to the pattern.

Now you've learnt to Kfb let's work the rest of this row. These instructions are written within *. This means that they are repeated. '*Kfb, K9* three times' means: Kfb, K9, Kfb, K9, Kfb, K9. When a pattern tells you to K followed by a number it's simply saying knit X number of stitches – here it's nine.

If you lose your place on the row you can follow the 'how to read the Kfb' instructions at the bottom of page 41.

At the end of the row a stitch count has been included (33 sts). 'Sts' is the abbreviation for stitches. This tells you the number of stitches you'll have at the end of the row. As you've increased using Kfb three times you'll have increased the stitch count by three from the 30 stitches that you cast on.

Row 4 K
Row 5 K
Row 6 K
The next three rows are all K rows, so just knit every row. You can use a row counter or download the tick sheet from firsttimeknits.com. There are tick sheets for each project, so you don't have to write in the book. I've also included examples on the next page of how to tell if you're about to work an odd or even row.

Row 7 *Kfb, K10* three times (36 sts)
This row is similar to Row 3 as it follows the same formula of increasing, followed by a number of stitches. You need to Kfb, K10, Kfb, K10, Kfb, K10.

Row 8 K
Row 9 K
Row 10 K
Knit these three rows.

Row 11 *Kfb, K11* three times (39 sts)

Once again you're increasing three times. Written in long hand that's Kfb, K11, Kfb, K11, Kfb, K11.

Row 12 K
Row 13 K
Row 14 K
Knit three more rows.

Row 15 Cast off, leaving a 30cm (12in) tail for sewing up.
If your memory needs refreshing, head to page 27 for the cast off tutorial.

Now knit the ears and nose of your animal. I've colour coded them to help.

BEAR EARS – make two
Cast on 4 stitches in M using 6mm (US 10) needles.
Row 1 K
Row 2 K
Row 3 *Kfb, K1* twice (6 sts)
On this row you're using Kfb again. The instructions are within *, so you'll need to repeat them. Written out that's Kfb, K1, Kfb, K1. At the end of the row you'll have increased from four to six stitches.
Row 4 K
Row 5 K
Row 6 K
Row 7 Cast off, leaving a 40cm (16in) tail for sewing up.

CAT OR FOX EARS – make two
Cast on 2 stitches in M using 6mm (US 10) needles.

Row 1 K
Row 2 K
Row 3 *Kfb* twice (4 sts)
On this row you're using Kfb again. These instructions are within *, so you'll need to repeat them. Written out that's Kfb, Kfb. At the end of the row you'll have increased from two to four stitches.
Row 4 K
Row 5 *Kfb, K1* twice (6 sts)
Row 6 K
Row 7 Cast off, leaving a 40cm (16in) tail for sewing up.

RABBIT EARS – make two
Cast on 2 stitches in M using 6mm (US 10) needles
Row 1 K
Row 2 K
Row 3 *Kfb* twice (4 sts)
On this row you're using Kfb again. These instructions are within *, so you'll need to repeat them. Written out that's Kfb, Kfb. At the end of the row you'll have increased from two to four stitches.
Row 4 K
Row 5 K
Row 6 K
Row 7 K
Row 8 K
Row 9 K
Row 10 K
Row 11 K
Row 12 K
Row 13 Cast off, leaving a 40cm (16in) tail for sewing up.

BEAR NOSE – make one
Cast on 3 stitches in C using 6mm (US 10) needles.
Row 1 K
Row 2 K
Row 3 Cast off, leaving a 40cm (16in) tail for sewing up.

CAT, FOX OR RABBIT NOSE – make one
Cast on 2 stitches in C using 6mm (US 10) needles.
Row 1 Kfb, K1 (3 sts)
Row 2 K
Row 3 Cast off, leaving a 40cm (16in) tail for sewing up.

SEWING UP
Fold the cup warmer so that it creates a tube and sew it up from the cast off edge down to the cast on edge using backstitch (see page 29). Turn it inside out – this will hide the sewing up seam.

Weave the loose ends of the cup warmer yarn into the seams. Don't weave in the tails of the ears and nose as you'll use them when sewing up.

See page 43 for further sewing up instructions. I've demonstrated sewing up on the bear, but you can follow the same instructions for the fox, cat and rabbit versions.

All the patterns also include sewing up instructions – for this one I've provided photographs as well.

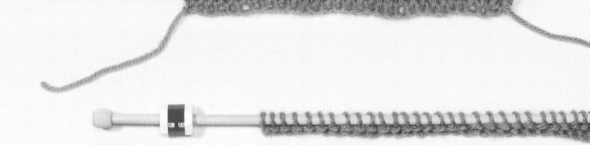

Odd row If your cast on tail is on the left, you're about to knit an odd-numbered row.

Even row If your cast on tail is on the right, you're about to knit an even-numbered row. If you're using a row counter it will be at the end of this needle.

Kfb increasing

More stitches please

'Kfb' means to knit into the front and the back of the same stitch. Broken down it's knit (K) into the front (f) and then into the back (b) of the same stitch. It increases a stitch from one to two stitches. There are other ways to increase stitches, but this is my preferred one. Kfb is similar to the knit stitch, but it also introduces knitting through the back of a stitch. So far we've only been knitting through the front, so it can be a little tricky to get this right.

Don't panic if you don't get it first time – you can always unravel the stitch and try again. Whenever a pattern asks you to Kfb, follow these instructions on just that stitch. Don't Kfb all the stitches, unless the pattern asks for it!

1. Knit through the front of the stitch, as you would with a regular knit stitch. If you're a continental knitter you can follow these instructions, but your hands will look different. There's an online video tutorial at firsttimeknits.com.

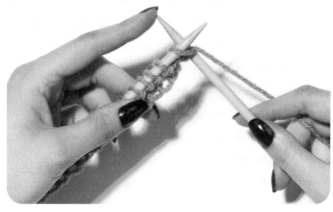

2. Wrap the yarn around the right needle, as you would with the knit stitch. For continental knitters, lay the yarn over the needle as you would with knit stitch. Begin to push the tip of the right needle with your left index finger.

3. Like the knit stitch, push the right needle down so that it catches the yarn wrapped around it, creating a new stitch.

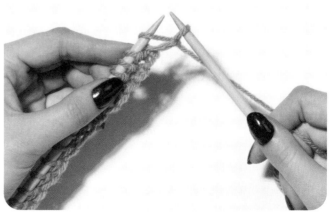

4. Instead of transferring the stitch off the left needle and onto the right, pull it gently away from the left needle.

5. Push the right needle through the back of the stitch you just knitted into on the left needle. This is the opposite side to where you would usually knit into.

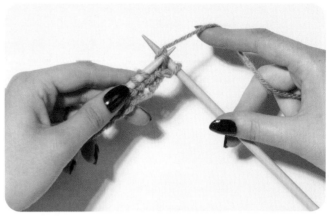

6. Just like the knit stitch, wrap the yarn around the right needle. If you're a continental knitter lay the yarn over the needle in the same way you would when knitting.

7. Again, using the same motion as the knit stitch, push the right needle down so that it catches the stitch, creating a new one. Then slide the stitch off the left needle and onto the right needle.

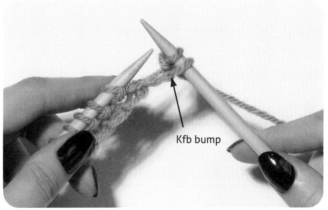

Kfb bump

8. Repeat Steps 1–7 every time you're asked to Kfb. A Kfb stitch is clearly distinguishable by the bump it creates on the left of the stitch. See below for my tip on reading the Kfb rows for Project 2.

How to read your knitting: Kfb rows

It can sometimes be hard to tell where you are on a Kfb row. If you get lost, just count your stitches. This photo shows how Row 3 will look after it's been worked. Row 3 is '*Kfb, K9* three times' – in long hand this row would be: Kfb, K9, Kfb, K9, Kfb, K9. The Kfb stitches create an extra bump, which can be hard to see on the knit row when the texture is all bumpy. I've highlighted every Kfb stitch on the row in the photo below. Remember when counting where you are in the middle of a row that Kfb counts as two stitches. After Row 3 you should have 33 stitches.

Project 2 mistakes

A little bit of help

I've just met my knitters for the second time. They started by making tension squares – this was a great way of refreshing their memory when it came to the knit stitch, and there were a few mistakes made along the way. If this happens to you, refer back to the Project 1 catch up pages. Over the first four projects, when you're learning a challenging new stitch, I've included catch up pages. I've highlighted a common mistake each knitter made and how we fixed it. If there's something you're stuck on that's not listed, head to the FAQ section at firsttimeknits.com.

Here Zoë has knitted into the front of the stitch twice creating two loops around the right needle. With the Kfb stitch knit into the front and then knit into the back of the same stitch. If you knit into the front twice, take the right needle out and pull the yarn to return the stitch to normal.

This is an incomplete Kfb stitch. Simon has knitted into the front, pushed the needle into the back and wrapped the yarn around it, but has not completed the stitch. Only part of the stitch has been knitted and the yarn is at the front. The best thing to do is to unravel the stitch and try to Kfb again.

Amala hasn't Kfb-ed quite right here – she's knitted into the stitch below (which we covered in the Project 1 catch up section) and then into the front of the stitch. It has added an extra stitch, but the hole isn't what we're after. Kfb is all about knowing the front and back of the stitch on the needle. She'll need to unravel the whole row and work it again.

Katie has knitted this piece beautifully, but there is an issue. She didn't follow the pattern properly. Following a pattern is a skill and it's easy to misunderstand instructions. Katie's tip is to check the stitch count after each row, especially when the pattern changes, to make sure it matches. If it doesn't then something is not quite right.

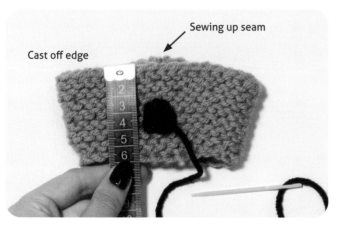

1. Place the warmer so that the sewing up seam is at the centre back. Make sure the widest part (the cast off edge) is at the top of the work. Place the nose in the centre, two ridges from the cast on edge, and sew in place using the cast off tail. Thread the cast off and cast on tails through the knit and tie them together on the wrong side to secure.

2. Measure two ridges above the top of the nose, in line with the right edge of the nose, and push the needle with the C cast off tail from the back of the work and out of the front. If you've run out of C yarn cut a new length and tie a knot at the end of it. Measure 2cm (¾in) to the right and push the needle through the knit to create a line.

3. This is your first eye. To make it sleepy find the centre point of the line and measure one ridge down. Push the needle from the back to the front of the knit at this point.

4. Pull the line down, then sew above the line and back into the work as shown. Mirror these instructions for the other eye. Then tie the two C yarn tails together and trim.

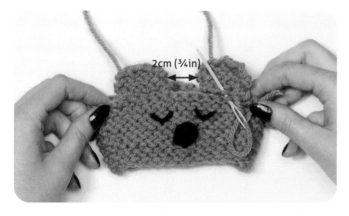

5. Place the cast off edges of the ears along the cast off edge, leaving a gap of 2cm (¾in) between them. Sew the left ear in place using the cast off tail. Sew through the cast off edge of the ear and into the cast off edge of the warmer. Repeat the sewing up instructions for the right ear.

6. On the wrong side, weave the cast off tails of the ears into the cast off edge of the warmer, using the same method as weaving into an inside seam. Thread the cast on tails through a darning needle and push them along the back of the ears, then weave them into the cast off seam.

Finished projects

How did they get on?

My knitters have just finished their second project. We spent two workshop sessions on Project 2: one knitting the tension squares and the second making the warmers. There were a few tension adjustments and some of the knitters had to make a second swatch before starting – it's all good practice though. If you end up with lots of tension squares you could always use them as coasters! All of my knitters picked a different shade of yarn and customized their cup warmers using my different design options. You can use these as inspiration or create your own.

Amala: The mug warmer built on skills learnt in the first project and introduced the Kfb stitch. When I tried this stitch I made some holes because I knitted into the wrong bit of the knitting, so I had to go back and try it again. I decided to knit a rabbit in yellow and changed the sewing on the eyes to give it happy eyes.

Katie: The Kfb was tricky at first as I knit quite tightly, but I improved with practice. I struggled at first reading the pattern and had to undo some of it, but on the second attempt I got it right. I enjoyed making the ears because they were quick and easy to attach. I wanted to make a fox because it matched my coffee cup.

Simon: I really enjoyed learning how to make the ears for this pattern. Sewing the eyes was a lesson in itself. I made two cup warmers because I wasn't happy with the first one as I sewed it up back to front. The making process was so quick that I felt I had another chance to improve on the first one.

Zoë: I found the mug warmer a bit harder, but once I mastered the Kfb increases it was great! I chose to knit a koala because if I were an animal that's what I'd be and I thought a little koala face would look so cute on a mug. I kept getting my tension wrong so it took a bit of trial and error before I could get the right stitch size.

Yarn

Yarn! What can I say about it? I could write a whole book on yarn, or at least about how to use it! Although it's often known as wool, I tend to use the term yarn as it's much broader and includes different fibre types.

So far I've recommended using acrylic yarns because they're affordable and when learning you're bound to make mistakes. Most patterns recommend a specific yarn, but that doesn't mean you have to use it. The great thing about making your own things is you can also choose which materials to use.

Wool is made from the fleeces of sheep and you'll find that there are plenty of sheep breeds to choose from. You'll see wool made from goats: there's cashmere and also mohair, which is from the angora goat. There's angora wool, which comes from the angora rabbit (which isn't confusing at all). You'll also find wool made from alpacas. Wool is usually hand wash only, but it will last a long time if you treat it right.

Acrylic yarns are what you've been working in so far. These are man-made fibres that are hardy, inexpensive and easy to use. They're great for making toys as you can usually machine wash them.

Cotton yarns are smooth yarns that are great for summer knits. You'll often see crochet patterns made in cotton as it's easier to use on a hook. As cotton yarns are non-elastic you may see them spun with other fibres to make them easier to use.

Mixed fibre yarns are spun using a mix of different materials. These blends can give the best of both worlds. By using a yarn that's a blend of wool and acrylic you may find it less itchy than using 100% wool.

Novelty yarns are fun yarns that are usually man made. They can be furry, bobbly, sparkly, made of paper or could be really unusual. The furry ones are appealing but as a beginner I'd suggest getting confident with knitting and purling before taking them on.

There are more and more yarn types becoming available and you'll soon learn which you prefer. You'll find shopping lists on the firsttimeknits.com website with different yarn options for each project, but you could also use yarnsub.com, a fantastic website for alternative yarns. Knitters also have their own social media platform, called Ravelry, which is another great site to check out for all your knitting needs.

Project 3:
Tiger scarf
Your first big project

My tiger scarf uses all of the skills that you've learnt so far and builds on them. It's knitted with super chunky yarn on big needles, so it'll grow quickly. This pattern also introduces decreasing and stripes – what more could you wish for! You can see my knitters' finished pieces on page 57 for some inspiration when choosing your colours.

Tiger scarf

MATERIALS

Plymouth Yarn Encore Mega yarn
(super chunky, 75% acrylic/25% wool,
58m per 100g):
**This pattern uses the same yarn as the
phone cosy. You can use the recommended
acrylic yarn or try another fibre.**
M (main colour) – Orange, 3 balls
B – Black, 1 ball
C – Cream, 1 ball

10mm (US 15) needles

Darning needle and row counter

FINISHED SIZE: 130cm (51in) long x 12.5cm
(5in) wide excluding legs and tail

TENSION

8 stitches x 14 rows = 10cm (4in) in garter stitch on 10mm (US 15) needles
using C. This tension is different to what is stated on the ball band, which is
8 stitches x 12 rows. As with Project 2, the pattern is asking for a different
tension, and I'll explain this later. Buy a yarn where the tension is 8 stitches x
12 rows, but you need to achieve a tension of 8 stitches x 14 rows.
You're making this tension swatch in garter stitch (knitting every row). This
pattern is asking you to swatch in C, as this knit uses several colours and
you'll have excess C. Make sure that you add 4 extra stitches and rows: cast
on 12 stitches, knit 18 rows and measure using the method on page 37.

ABBREVIATIONS

K Knit
Kfb Knit into the front and back of the same stitch (increase)
SKP Slip a stitch, knit a stitch and pass the slipped stitch over (decrease)
K2tog Knit two stitches together (decrease)
(sts) Stitches: The number of stitches you'll have at the end of the row
This pattern introduces two new abbreviations: SKP and K2tog.

My tiger scarf is knitted in one large
piece, starting from the bottom and
finishing at the face. The ears, legs and
tail are then sewn on later.
With this pattern there are annotations
along the way. These will help to build
your pattern reading skills.

SCARF – make one
Cast on 10 stitches in M.
There are lots of rows in this pattern!
You can use a row counter or download
the tick sheet from firsttimeknits.com.

Row 1 K
As with Project 2, the good stuff, like
increasing, decreasing and colour
changing, will happen on the odd rows.

Row 2 K
Row 3 K
Row 4 K
Row 5 K
Row 6 K
Row 7 K
Row 8 K
At this point you'll have worked eight
garter stitch rows – that's four ridges.

Row 9 Change to B, working all stitches
in it until stated. K
Colour changing is your first new
technique. The pattern is asking you to
change to B and to work every stitch in
it until stated. It then says 'K', so you
should knit every stitch in the row. See
page 50 for how to change colour to B.

Row 10 K
Row 11 Change to M, working all
stitches in it until stated. K
The pattern is asking for another
colour change (see Step 4 on page 50).

Row 12 K
Row 13 K
At this point you need to carry the B
yarn with you (see Step 5 on page 51).

Row 14 K
Row 15 Change to B, working all
stitches in it until stated. K
Change to B (see Step 6 on page 51).

Row 16 K
Rows 1–16 create a repeat (see below).

The stripe repeat

Rows 1–16 make up the stripe repeat. The colour changes
for the repeat will always happen at the start of an odd-
numbered row. This is because the stripes create a pattern
on the back of the work. This is the first knit where you'll
have a right and wrong side, as the last two projects were
reversible. The repeat will look correct when then scarf is
facing the right way.

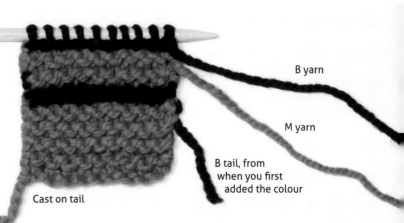

B yarn

M yarn

B tail, from
when you first
added the colour

Cast on tail

The wrong side

This is the wrong side of the work. You can see how the colour change has created a pattern in the back of the work. Be careful not to change colour on the wrong side of the stripe repeat.

Repeat Rows 1–16 nine more times. You'll have 10 sets of repeats in total. Patterns often work in repeats, which saves space. When there's a repeat in a pattern it'll be written in short hand. Here you need to repeat Rows 1–16 nine more times.

You can either use a row counter, resetting it back to 0 at the end of each repeat, or download my tick sheet. After each repeat you don't need to cast off the knitting; just continue working the piece. The row after the end of the repeat will become Row 1.

I've written the repeat below without any annotations. Remember to carry the yarn with you up the side of the piece as you work the repeat.

Row 1 Change to M, working all stitches in it until stated. K
Row 2 K
Row 3 K
Row 4 K
Row 5 K
Row 6 K
Row 7 K
Row 8 K
Row 9 Change to B, working all stitches in it until stated. K
Row 10 K
Row 11 Change to M, working all stitches in it until stated. K
Row 12 K
Row 13 K
Row 14 K
Row 15 Change to B, working all stitches in it until stated. K
Row 16 K
After working the 10 repeats, reset the row counter back to 0.

As with the repeats, you need to set your row counter back to 0 before working the next part of the pattern.

Row 1 Change to M, working all stitches in it until stated. K. From this point don't carry the B yarn with you; instead cut it, leaving a tail for weaving in.
Row 2 K
Row 3 K
Row 4 K
Row 5 Kfb, K7, Kfb, K1 (12 sts)
Kfb is used here (see page 40 to refresh your memory).

Row 6 K
Row 7 K
Row 8 K
Row 9 K
Row 10 K
Row 11 K
Row 12 K
Row 13 K
Row 14 K
Row 15 SKP, K8, K2tog (10 sts)
Here the two new stitch techniques are introduced – both decrease the work. Head to page 52 to work the SKP stitch on the first two stitches of the row.

Once you've decreased using SKP, knit eight stitches as usual. Then head to page 53 to learn how to K2tog on the last two stitches on the row.

You'll have decreased the work by two stitches and should now have ten stitches on your needle. You've just learnt to decrease! We'll be using these techniques on some of the upcoming rows too.

Row 16 K

Row 17 SKP, K6, K2tog (8 sts)
You're decreasing again here, so SKP the first two stitches, then knit the next six stitches and decrease the final two stitches using K2tog. You'll now have eight stitches on the needle.

Row 18 K
Row 19 K
Row 20 K
Row 21 SKP, K4, K2tog (6 sts)
It's another set of decreases – you know what to do!

Row 22 K
Row 23 Change to C, working all stitches in it until stated. K
Here you need to change to C (the other colour in the pattern). Add it to the work in the same way as the B yarn (see page 50).

Row 24 K
Row 25 Kfb, K3, Kfb, K1 (8 sts)
Row 26 K
Row 27 Kfb, K5, Kfb, K1 (10 sts)
Row 28 K
Row 29 Kfb, K7, Kfb, K1 (12 sts)
Row 30 K
Row 31 K
Row 32 Change to B, working all stitches in it until stated. K
Attach the B yarn, as you did at the start of the repeat. Here you'll notice that the colour change is happening on an even row (the wrong side). As a general rule patterns will give you instructions on an odd row (the right side), but here I'm breaking that rule. Trust the pattern and all will be revealed later.

Row 33 K

Row 34 Change to C, working all stitches in it until stated. K. Carry the B yarn up the side of the work.
Bring the C yarn behind the B yarn and knit with it.

Row 35 K
Row 36 Kfb, K9, Kfb, K1 (14 sts)
Carry the B yarn up the work.

Row 37 K
Row 38 Change to B, working all stitches in it until stated. K
Bring the B yarn under the C yarn and knit with it.

Row 39 K
Row 40 Change to C, working all stitches in it until stated. K
Row 41 K
Row 42 K
Don't forget to carry the B yarn!

Row 43 K
Row 44 Change to B, working all stitches in it until stated. K
Row 45 K
Row 46 Change to C, working all stitches in it from here on. K

Row 47 K
Row 48 SKP, K10, K2tog (12 sts)
Row 49 K
Row 50 SKP, K8, K2tog (10 sts)
Row 51 K
Row 52 Cast off.

EARS – make two in B and two in C
Here the pattern is asking you to use different colours. Knit two ears in B and two in C.
Cast on 5 stitches.
Row 1 K
Row 2 K
Row 3 K
Row 4 K
Row 5 SKP, K1, K2tog (3 sts)
Row 6 K
Row 7 Cast off.

LEGS – make four
Cast on 4 stitches in M.
Rows 1–18 Work in garter stitch.
Garter stitch is the term for knitting every row. Knit 18 rows – that's nine ridges in total.
Row 19 K1, K2tog, K1 (3 sts)
Row 20 K
Row 21 Cast off

TAIL – make one
Cast on 3 stitches in M.
Row 1 K
Row 2 K
Row 3 K
Row 4 K
Row 5 Change to B, working all stitches in it until stated. K
Row 6 K
Row 7 Change to C, working all stitches in it until stated. K. Carry the B yarn.
Row 8 K
Row 9 K
Row 10 K
Rows 11–22 Repeat Rows 5–10 two more times.
The pattern is asking you to repeat Rows 5–10 twice.

Row 23 Change to B, working all stitches in it from here on. K. Cut the C yarn, as you won't need it again.
Row 24 K
Row 25 K1, K2tog (2 sts)
Row 26 K
Row 27 Cast off.

SEWING UP
See page 54 for the sewing up tutorial.

What to do when you run out of yarn

At some point in this project, you're going to run out of yarn. When this happens you'll need to add a new ball. Adding new yarn should be done at the start of a row. When you come to the end of a ball it can be tempting to knit another row, only to find that you run out halfway.

To work out whether you have

enough to knit a row, pull the end of the yarn across the top of the row, back to the start and then across again, zigzagging it over the piece. If there's enough yarn to do this, you can knit the row. If there's not, then you need to add the next ball.

Follow the instructions on page 50 to add a new ball.

Changing colour

Adding stripes

One of the things I love about craft is how you can customize your knits to make them unique. Changing the colours is a great way of adding your own personality to a pattern. Here you'll be using a really simple way of adding in a new colour at the start of a row. I designed the tiger scarf to have a stripe repeat, so you'll be adding a new colour and working the stripes from the pattern. You'll also be carrying the colours with you. This means that every time you want to use the other colour it'll be there ready to use, rather than having to add a new piece each time. By carrying the yarn you won't have lots of tails to weave in at the end of the piece, which you'll be very grateful for!

1. Once you reach the row where you need to change colour, which is Row 9 of the tiger scarf, measure approximately 40cm (16in) of the new yarn colour. Wrap the new yarn around the old colour and tie it in a knot.

2. Slide the knot up the tail of the old yarn to the first stitch on the row. Keep the old yarn attached to the knitting – don't cut it off as you'll be using it later. Don't worry about the tail of the B yarn either, as you'll weave it in at the end.

3. Then just start knitting with the new colour – adding a colour is as easy as that! You can also use this method if you run out and have to add a new ball to the work. For the tiger scarf knit Rows 9 and 10 in B.

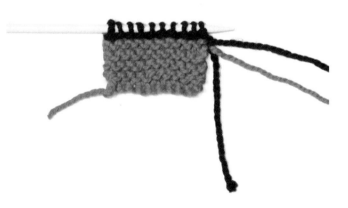

4. Once you've knitted these rows the piece will look like this. Row 11 says: 'Change to M, working all stitches in it until stated. K. You don't need to cut the yarns and reattach them; instead you will carry the colours up the work.

5. As the M yarn is only a ridge below the B yarn, you can start knitting with it. Use this as a rule when knitting in stripes. Move the M yarn behind the B yarn and knit Rows 11 and 12 in M.

6. Rows 13 and 14 are knitted in M. As you're working more than one ridge in M you need to bring the B yarn with you. If you leave it behind and then knit with it later there will be a long loop on the side of the work.

7. All you have to do is twist the B yarn under and then over the top of the M yarn, then start knitting with the M yarn. Be careful not to pull the B yarn too tightly as it can gather the edge of the work. Knit Rows 13 and 14 in M.

8. Row 15 says: 'Change to B, working all stitches in it until stated. K'. Here you need to change back to B. As you've been carrying this colour with you, just bring it behind the M yarn and start knitting with it. Knit Rows 15 and 16 in B.

9. Rows 1–16 create the stripe repeat. You need to repeat these rows nine more times, so you'll have ten sets of stripe repeats in total. As your first row is knitted in M, bring the M yarn up from behind the B yarn and start knitting with it.

10. Rows 1–8 of the repeat are all knitted in M. Remember to carry the B yarn with you, as you did in Step 7, every time you start an odd row. If you do forget to carry it, you can cut the yarn and add it by tying it on, as shown in Steps 1–3.

SKP decreasing

Slip a stitch, knit a stitch, pass the slipped stitch over

SKP is a decrease stitch – it's used to reduce two stitches to one stitch. Written in long hand it's 'slip a stitch, knit a stitch, and then pass the slipped stitch over'. It can also be written as 'sl1 k1 psso', but I prefer to say SKP. You'll find there are different kinds of decrease stitches, but this one creates a left-leaning decrease. It's very similar to casting off but, unlike casting off, SKP can occur at any part of the row. When you see SKP, follow these steps.

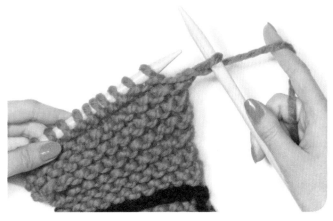

1. SKP reduces two stitches to one. Firstly, slip a stitch from the left to the right needle. You don't need to knit it; just transfer it from the left to the right needle.

2. Knit the next stitch on the left needle as usual. The slipped stitch and the stitch you've just knitted are the two stitches you'll be using to decrease.

3. As with casting off (see page 27), push the left needle tip through the front of the slipped stitch. The needles will cross with the left on top of the right. Place your left index finger on the tip of the right needle.

4. Use the left needle to slide the slipped stitch over the knitted stitch, transferring it over and then off the needle. This decreases the work by one stitch and creates a decrease that leans towards the left of the piece.

K2tog decreasing
Knit two stitches together

K2tog is also a decrease stitch, used to reduce two stitches to one stitch. It's doing the same thing as SKP, just in a different way. K2tog literally means 'knit two stitches together'. It's the most common decrease stitch you'll come across in the knitting world and one of the easiest. K2tog creates a right-leaning decrease – the opposite to SKP. Apply the technique shown below every time you're asked to K2tog in a pattern.

1. Work the row up to the point you're asked to K2tog. Every time you K2tog you'll be applying it to two stitches on the left needle.

2. As with the knit stitch, you'll push the right needle from the front to the back of the stitch. However, instead of doing this to one stitch, you'll apply it to both at the same time.

3. Use the same action as for the knit stitch: for the English method wrap the yarn around the right needle, and for the continental method lay the yarn that you are holding with your left finger over the needle tip.

4. Push the right needle down so that it catches the yarn, creating a new stitch. Slide the old stitches off the left needle. You'll have knitted the two stitches together and created a decrease that leans towards the right.

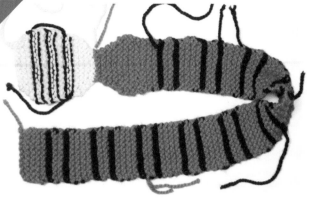

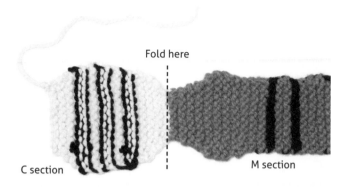

Fold here

C section

M section

1. This is how the main part of the scarf will look once it's finished. You'll have made a few tails along the way and you'll need to weave them in. As the scarf doesn't have an inside seam, you'll need to weave the tails into the wrong side of the knit (see page 56 for the tutorial).

2. Find the M and C colour change. The colour C section looks wrong compared to the M section. Don't worry – this is how it's supposed to look! Fold the scarf back on itself at the colour change point, so that the right side of the C section is facing the wrong side of the M section.

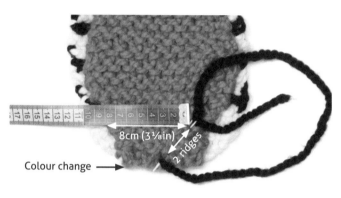

8cm (3⅛in)

Colour change

2 ridges

3. Knot the end of a length of M yarn and thread it through a darning needle. Push the needle through the cast off edge, from the back to the front. **Only** sew one side of the face with a backstitch. Keep the stitches small, so the yarn does not show too much on the M side. It will show on the C section.

4. For the nose, thread a 60cm (24in) length of B yarn through a darning needle and tie a knot at the end. Push it from the wrong side of the M section through to the centre of the snout, one ridge from the colour change. Measure two ridges up and 8cm (3⅛in) from the left side, and sew into the face.

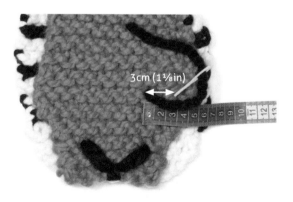

3cm (1⅛in)

5. Move the needle along the wrong side of the work and out of the centre of the snout where it first exited. Mirror the instructions for the left side. Repeat Steps 4 and 5 again to make the nose thicker. Add a small vertical line in the centre of the nose down to the colour change.

6. Measure six ridges from the colour change, in line with the edge of the nose, and sew the B yarn from the back of the work. Measure 3cm (1⅛in) to the right and sew a line, then make it sleepy, as you did in Steps 2 and 3 on page 43 for the cup warmer. Mirror these instructions for the left eye.

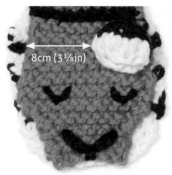

Colour change

7. Place a C and B ear together, matching the shape of the knit, with the cast on edges (the widest parts) together. Sew them together using backstitch in C. Leave the cast on edges open, turn inside out and weave the tails into the seam. Repeat for the second ear.

8. With the C side of the first ear facing you, place it nine ridges up from the colour change and 8cm (3⅛in) from the left side of the piece. Place the ear so that it's at a slight diagonal angle and sits with the cast on edges open – this will help to keep it upright. Pin in place.

9. Sew in place using the C yarn. Sew through the cast on edge of the ear and into the knit of the head, being careful not to sew through the folded C section. Sew all around the ear, leaving the cast on edges slightly open – this will keep the ear upright.

10. Mirror Step 8 for the other ear. There will be a gap of about 2cm (¾in) in the centre between the top of the ears. Sew the ear in place using C, keeping the cast on edges open to keep it upright, and weave in the loose ends on the wrong side of the piece.

11. Sew up the other side of the face, mirroring the instructions in Step 3. Turn the piece so that it's facing the other way and place the cast on edge of the leg along the B stripe closest to the colour change. Sew in place using M. Repeat for the second leg on the other side of the scarf.

12. Place the cast on edges of the back legs along the cast on edge of the scarf, with the cast on edge of the tail in the centre. Sew all three in place using M. Sew through the edges to secure in place. Weave in all loose ends using the technique on page 56.

Weaving in

What to do with all those loose ends

At the end of your knitting project you'll be asked to 'weave in the loose ends'. So far you've been weaving in through the inside seams of the work. However, if there's not a seam available, like with your tiger scarf, you'll need to weave the loose ends into the knit itself. When weaving in it's good to read the knit first. By understanding the piece it'll make the weaving in instructions much clearer. Your tiger scarf has three different colours to weave in – I've used C to demonstrate, but you can apply this technique to any of the colours on the wrong side of the piece.

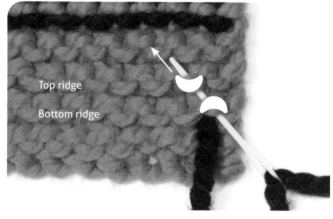

1. When you first read your knitting I showed you the ridges along the work. Now look at the ridges again – along the top of each ridge the stitches look like frowns, and along the bottom they look like smiles. As garter stitch is reversible, always weave in on the wrong side of the piece.

2. Thread the yarn tail through a darning needle. Find the ridge closest to where the tail starts and push the needle through the frown on that ridge. Let's call this the 'below ridge'. Then push it diagonally into the smile on the ridge above it (labelled as the 'above ridge' in the photo).

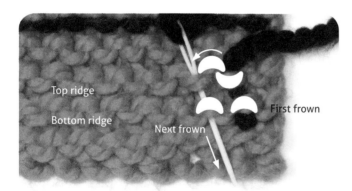

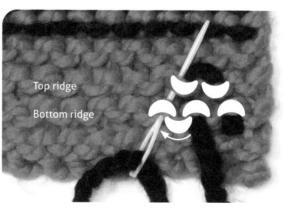

3. Push the needle and yarn out of the smile, follow the frown next to it and sew into the smile after the frown. Push the needle diagonally into the next frown on the below ridge. Don't pull the yarn too tightly – let it naturally follow the shape of the stitches.

4. Push the needle and yarn out of the frown on the below ridge, follow the smile next to it and push it through the next frown and diagonally towards the previous smile on the above ridge. Repeat Steps 3 and 4 several times along the stitches and then trim the yarn.

Finished projects

How did they get on?

The tiger scarf was my knitters' first big project. I haven't included a catch up section because any mistakes that my knitters made and how to fix them were covered in Projects 1 and 2. You can refer to these pages at any point and if you get really stuck you can head to the FAQ section at firsttimeknits.com for some additional help. My knitters started their tiger scarves at the studio and took them home to work on once they were confident with the stripe repeat. It was lovely to see how quickly their projects grew and to see how each finished knit had its own personality.

Amala: There were so many stripes! Once I got used to the pattern it was fine though. I chose to knit a white tiger and made it longer by adding an extra two repeats. It's a knit that you shouldn't try to do in one go, as you'll be seeing stripes for days! It's worth it though, because the chunky yarn is so cosy and warm.

Katie: I really enjoyed knitting the actual scarf as it came together so quickly. It was fun to understand how to add a colour. It was nice to go back to the yarn and big needles from the first project too. I found sewing the parts together a challenge, especially the ears, but seeing its really adorable face made it worth it!

Simon: This pattern was a real education in weaving in. At first it was challenging but in the end it felt like second nature. Learning the decreasing techniques was the highlight and I thought the ears were cute. I chose the colours because they complemented each other and were a polarized version of the original design.

Zoë: As this was a big project I found it tougher than the first two. I made the mistake of leaving it and coming back to it, so I felt it wasn't as consistent as the smaller projects. I then sewed up the wrong side, so my bad! I chose colours that complemented each other and didn't stray too far from the original tiger stripes.

Project 4:
Bottle carrier

Hello purl...

My whale water bottle carrier is the perfect project for introducing purl. Now you can knit, you can definitely purl. I chose this project as I always have a bottle of water with me, but really dislike taking a big bag just to carry it. A whale felt very fitting for this design, as by using a reusable bottle there'll be a bit less single-use plastic. Win!

Stocking stitch tension

Relax, it's just a square

Of course Project 4 starts with a tension square. But this one is exciting, as you're going to learn how to purl!

I recommend Rico Fashion Jersey, a chunky yarn, here. You'll also need a tape measure, some pins and needles in the following sizes: 6mm, 7mm, 8mm (US 10, 10½, 11). See the materials list on page 65 for more information.

So far you've been checking your tension by knitting in garter stitch. However, when purling is introduced you can knit a row and purl a row alternately – this is called stocking stitch. It creates a smooth fabric on one side with bumps on the other. This is why most knitting patterns are written in rows of two, because you'll knit one way and purl back, making a right and wrong side. With your

previous swatches, I've been asking you to follow the tension I've given you, not the one on the ball band. This is because the ball band tension is usually written in stocking stitch. When knitting and purling alternately the stitch shape changes, creating longer stitches. You'll be asked to achieve the right tension using a certain stitch.

When knitting in stocking stitch you'll have a right side and a wrong side. The right side features a smooth fabric. Each stitch on the right side looks like a 'V', and these 'V's build on top of each other to make the rows. On the wrong side you'll find a bumpy fabric, which looks a like garter stitch, but is actually called reverse stocking stitch.

The tension for Project 4 is 16 stitches x 23 rows on 7mm (US 10½) needles.

To learn how to purl and make your swatch, see page 60.

As with a garter stitch swatch, you will measure the stitches and rows on the right side. Using a pin, mark the side of a V stitch, two stitches from the edge, and measure 10cm (4in) horizontally, counting the V stitches within the 0–10cm (0–4in) area – you should have 16. Mark the top of a V stitch, two stitches under the cast off edge, with a pin and measure 10cm (4in) vertically, counting the V rows that sit on top of each other – you should have 23.

If your swatch has too many stitches, go up a needle size to 8mm (US 11). If it's too loose and there aren't enough stitches, go down to 6mm (US 10). Once you've achieved the right tension you can start making the whale on page 65.

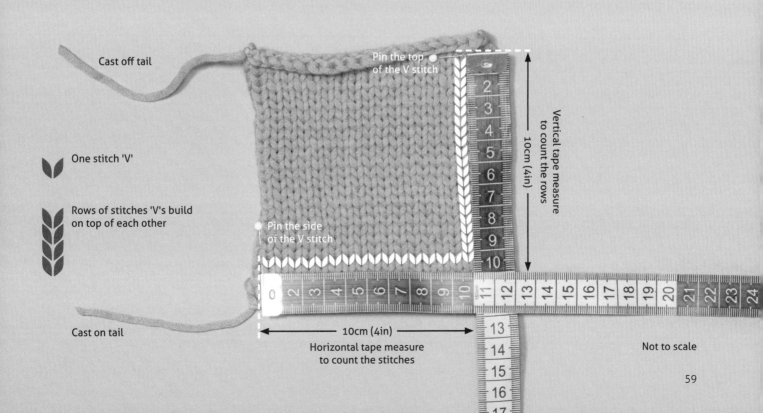

Cast off tail

Pin the top of the V stitch

One stitch 'V'

Rows of stitches 'V's build on top of each other

Pin the side of the V stitch

Vertical tape measure to count the rows

10cm (4in)

Cast on tail

10cm (4in)

Horizontal tape measure to count the stitches

Not to scale

59

Purl stitch

What's all the fuss about?

Purl is similar to the knit stitch, but at the same time it's almost the opposite. These instructions explain the English method, but the continental method can be seen on page 62. These steps show you how to purl and make a swatch. You'll soon find that knitting and purling are almost always used together in alternate rows – this is called stocking stitch (also known as stockinette or plain stitch). This stitch is the most recognisable type of knitted fabric. It's smooth on one side, bumpy on the other and the edges curl. Unlike garter stitch, patterns very rarely use only the purl stitch, so if you're purling, the knit stitch will probably be used alongside it. Grab your M yarn and a pair of 7mm (US 10½) needles. The tension is 16 stitches x 23 rows, so cast on 4 more stitches – that's 20.

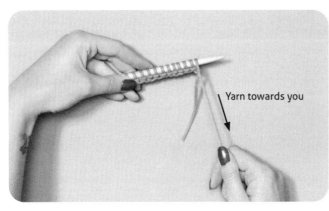

Yarn towards you

1. After you've cast on 20 stitches, knit your first row as usual. Turn the needle ready to work Row 2 – this is the side you're going to purl. With purling the most important thing is to make sure that the yarn is pulled towards you, unlike the knit stitch where the yarn is always behind the needles.

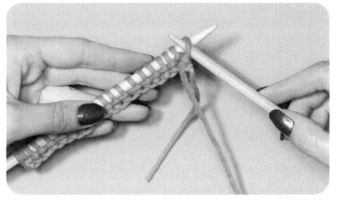

2. As with the knit stitch, find the stitch above the bump. But unlike knitting, push the right needle from the back to the front of the stitch. The needles will cross, with the right over the left – this is the opposite way to how they've been when working the knit stitch.

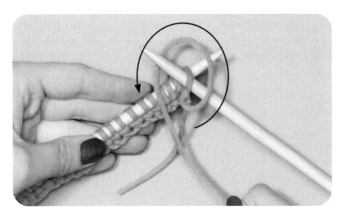

3. Wrap the yarn anti-clockwise over the right needle and around the tip of it, so that it's sitting between both needles. Be careful not to wrap the cast on tail around the needle by accident. Trim the tail if it's too long.

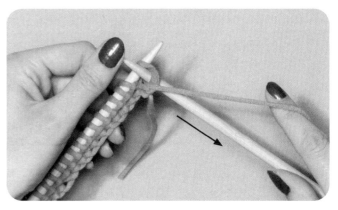

4. Pull the wrapped yarn, so that it sits naturally between the needles – as always, don't pull it too tightly. Using your left thumb, push the right needle tip down and away from you, so that it catches the wrapped yarn.

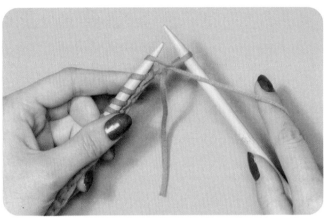

5. Be careful not to lose the wrapped yarn. This is the trickiest part of purling. If you do, just start again, repeating Steps 2–4.

6. As with the knit stitch, catching the wrapped yarn creates a new stitch on the right needle. Pull the right needle away from the left.

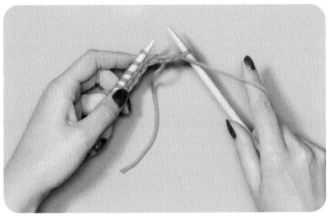

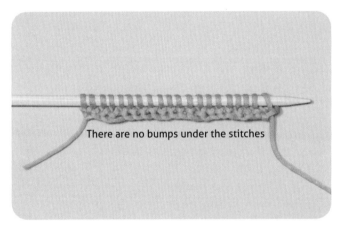

There are no bumps under the stitches

7. Slide the stitch off the left needle. You've just purled! Repeat Steps 2–7 for every stitch on the row. To keep your tension even, remember to wrap the yarn around your hand in the same way you do when knitting (see page 16). At the end of the row the fabric will look bumpy.

8. Turn the work so that the right side is facing you. Notice how the work is smooth, there are no bumps under the loops on the needle and the stitches look like 'V's – this is the big change from garter stitch. This is an odd row, so knit it, making sure the yarn is behind the needle.

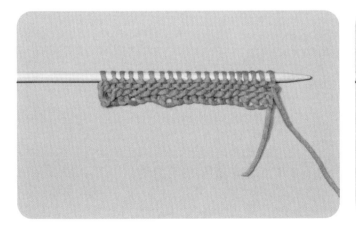

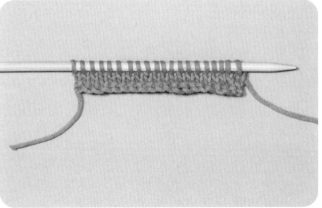

9. After knitting the row, turn the work and purl the next one, which will be an even row. As the work grows you'll notice the difference in the fabric. When the wrong side (an even row) is facing you, the fabric is bumpy, so purl that row.

10. Work in stocking stitch, knitting a row and then purling a row until you have 28 rows. If you need any help with purling, head to page 64 to see how my knitters got on. Cast off and return to page 59 to measure your swatch.

Continental purl stitch

Purling European style

If you've come from the English purl page you'll know that your first task of Project 4 is to make a tension square. As a continental knitter, you'll be a continental purler too, so follow this method to make your swatch. If you knit using the English method, head back to page 60. When you're asked to purl you'll find that you've probably worked a knit row first, as knit and purl are often used alternately. Knitting a row followed by purling a row is called stocking stitch, which creates the most recognisable type of knitted fabric.

It's smooth on one side and bumpy on the other. You're going to have a go at making it now. Grab your M yarn and a pair of 7mm (US 10½) needles. The tension is 16 stitches x 23 rows, so cast on 4 more stitches – that's 20. Use a row counter to help you to keep track.

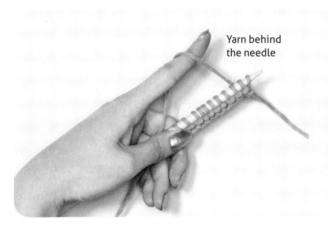

Yarn behind the needle

1. After you've cast on 20 stitches, knit your first row as usual. Turn the needle ready to work Row 2 – on this side you're going to learn to purl. After the knit row, your hand will be in the continental position with the yarn behind the needle.

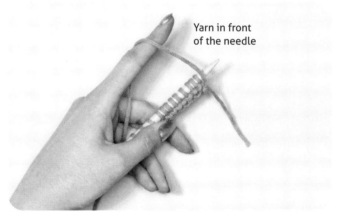

Yarn in front of the needle

2. When purling, the yarn has to be in front of the needle, otherwise you'll accidentally add another stitch. All you have to do is move the yarn in front of the needle with your hand still in the continental position.

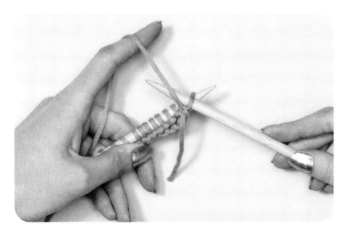

3. Push the right needle from the back to the front of the stitch above the bump. The needles will cross with the right over the left. The yarn will also be in front of the needle.

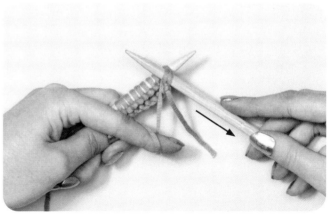

4. Move your left index finger down so that the yarn wraps around the right needle tip. This can feel a little awkward at first. This is why the yarn has to be at the front when purling.

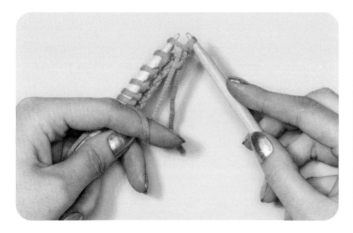

5. Using your right hand, move the right needle down and away from you, so that it catches the wrapped stitch. Keep your finger in the same downward position. If you lose the wrapped stitch, just repeat Steps 2–5 again.

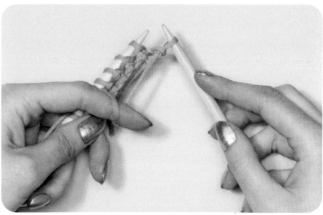

6. Catching the wrapped yarn creates a new stitch on the right needle. Pull the right needle away from the left one and, as with the knit stitch, slide the old stitch off the left needle. You've just purled!

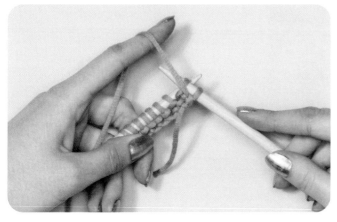

7. Push the right needle from the back to the front of the next stitch. Then move your left index finger back up so that the yarn moves over the right needle tip. Repeat Steps 4–7 every time you need to purl. Purl every stitch on Row 2.

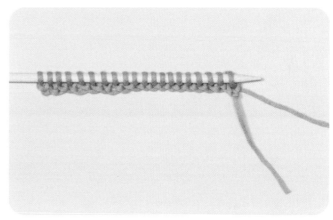

8. At the end of the row the fabric will look like garter stitch as it will be bumpy. Turn the work around, with the right side (an odd row) facing you. Notice how there are no bumps and the work is smooth. Knit this row.

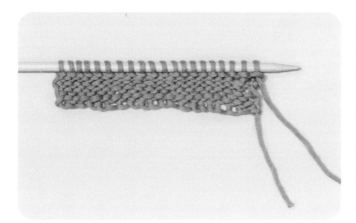

9. After knitting Row 3, turn the work and purl Row 4. As the work grows you'll start to notice that the fabric looks different on each side. When the wrong side (an even row) is facing you, the fabric is bumpy, so purl that row.

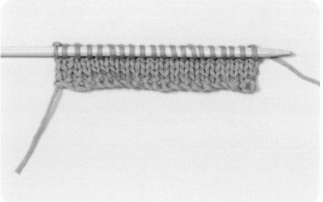

10. Work in stocking stitch, knitting a row and then purling a row, until you have 28 rows. If you need any help with purling, head to page 64 to see how my knitters got on. Cast off and return to page 59 to measure your swatch.

Purl mistakes

A little bit of help

Like you, my knitters have mastered the knit stitch, increasing and decreasing now, so I thought this was the right time to introduce purl. I've documented the mistakes they made while making their swatches. At first, everyone seemed a little daunted by the idea of purling, but once they got into it they could do the purl stitch without any real issues. There were a few mistakes but, as you'll see, there were less issues than when they first learnt to knit. I've also included a catch up page that looks at the mistakes made while knitting the whale project on page 69.

When purling you need to wrap the yarn around the needle anti-clockwise, but here Katie has wrapped it clockwise. This will still make a purl stitch but it will twist it. I've included fixing tips for twisted stitches on page 72 if you come across any, but it's best to wrap the yarn around the correct way.

Simon has made one of the most common mistakes. As you can see, there's a bumpy row across the work. That's because he's either knitted on a purl row or purled on a knit row. This mistake was made a few rows ago, so he'll have to unravel to fix it (see page 70 for the tutorial).

Zoë thought that, as you purled from the back to the front of the stitch, she'd need to go through the back of the knit stitch. By pushing the needle through the back of the loops this twists the stitches. Fix the occasional twisted stitch using the tutorial on page 72. If you find that several rows are twisted, you'll need to unravel them (see page 70).

Here Amala has an incomplete stitch on a purl row – this means that she didn't finish the stitch on the knit row before. In the same way as when working in garter stitch, this has created an extra, odd-looking stitch. You can see how to fix this on page 24. This tutorial also includes advice for fixing incomplete stitches on a knit row.

Whale water bottle carrier

MATERIALS

Rico Fashion Jersey yarn (chunky, 64% cotton/36% polyamide, 72m per 50g): Knitting doesn't have to be wool! I've picked a cotton blend for this project. You can also knit with acrylic – find my substitution list in the Project 4 section at firsttimeknits.com.

M (main colour) – Blue, 2 balls
B (strap colour) – Navy, 1 ball
C (under piece colour) – Cream, 1 ball

Small needles: 6mm (US 10)
Large needles: 7mm (US 10½)
You will need two different needle sizes. The pattern will refer to the needles as small or large instead of giving the size.

Darning needle, white and black felt, white cotton and sewing needle

TENSION

16 stitches x 23 rows = 10cm (4in) in St st on 7mm (US 10½) needles
Your first task was to make a tension swatch in M (see page 59). Ensure that you cast on 4 more stitches and work 4 more rows. Here the pattern is asking you to work in St st (see abbreviations list below).

ABBREVIATIONS

K Knit
Kfb Knit into the front and back of the same stitch (increase)
SKP Slip a stitch, knit a stitch and pass the slipped stitch over (decrease)
K2tog Knit two stitches together (decrease)
... Repeat the instructions within the asterisks
P Purl
(sts) Stitches: The number of stitches you'll have at the end of the row
St st Stocking stitch: Knit a row, purl a row alternately
You'll notice that there are two new abbreviations: P and St st.

FINISHED SIZE: Holds a 500ml (17oz) reusable water bottle

This project introduces purl within a pattern. You've just practised purling with your tension swatch, where you knitted a row, followed by purling a row, which is called stocking stitch. Make the tail first, as it's a small piece that uses stocking stitch as well as some increasing and decreasing. After making the tail, knit the top piece. The fins, strap and under piece introduce a new technique, so we'll knit those last.

TAIL – make one

Cast on 10 stitches in M using the large needles.

Use the larger needles to cast on. If your tension was correct with 7mm (US 10½) needles, use those. If you changed needle sizes, use the size you achieved the correct tension with.

Row 1 K
Just like with the previous projects, all the good stuff, like increasing and decreasing, happens on the odd rows.

Row 2 P
P is the abbreviation for purl. If you need some help with purling, head back to page 60. By knitting a row and then purling a row, you're creating a stocking stitch fabric. My knitters used the term 'purl back' for the even rows, so they'd knit an odd row and then purl back, ready to work the next odd row.

Row 3 K
Row 4 P
Row 5 K
Row 6 P
Row 7 K
Row 8 P
Row 9 K2, Kfb, K3, Kfb, K3 (12 sts)
Here you've got some increasing. As stocking stitch fabric is smooth on the right side you'll notice the Kfb stitches more. They create bumps on the left part of the Kfb stitch. You couldn't really see them when working in garter stitch, but they're perfectly normal. I've highlighted these stitches on the photo at the top of page 66.

Row 10 P
Row 11 K2, Kfb, K1, Kfb, K1, Kfb, K1, Kfb, K3 (16 sts)
Row 12 P
Row 13 K2, Kfb, K2, Kfb, K3, Kfb, K2, Kfb, K3 (20 sts)
Row 14 P
Row 15 K2, Kfb, K3, Kfb, K5, Kfb, K3, Kfb, K3 (24 sts)
Row 16 P
Row 17 K2, Kfb, K4, Kfb, K7, Kfb, K4, Kfb, K3 (28 sts)
Row 18 P
Row 19 K
Row 20 P
Row 21 K
Row 22 P
Row 23 K
Row 24 P
Row 25 K2, SKP, K3, SKP, K10, K2tog, K3, K2tog, K2 (24 sts)
Here you're decreasing again. Head back to page 52 if you need some help with the SKP and K2tog stitches.

Row 26 P
Row 27 K2, SKP, K2, SKP, K8, K2tog, K2, K2tog, K2 (20 sts)
Row 28 P
Row 29 K2, SKP, K1, SKP, K6, K2tog, K1, K2tog, K2 (16 sts)
As with increasing, the decrease stitches also create patterns in the work. I've included advice on how to read them on the image overleaf.

Row 30 P
Row 31 K2, SKP, SKP, K4, K2tog, K2tog, K2 (12 sts)
Row 32 P

Increasing and decreasing

As you start increasing you'll notice bumps in the fabric – these are the Kfb stitches. Every Kfb will make a bump on the left of the increased stitch. This is totally normal. I've circled the first set of increases on Row 9, but you can also see them on Rows 11 and 13.

From Row 25 you'll be decreasing using SKP and K2tog. These stitches will also show when working in stocking stitch. On the row below an SKP, the slipped stitch that's transferred over the knit stitch moves to the left, making it a left-leaning decrease. I've highlighted two SKP stitches on the right of the work. K2tog mirrors SKP, as it's a right-leaning decrease. The stitches on the row below the K2tog move to the right as they've been decreased – I've highlighted these too.

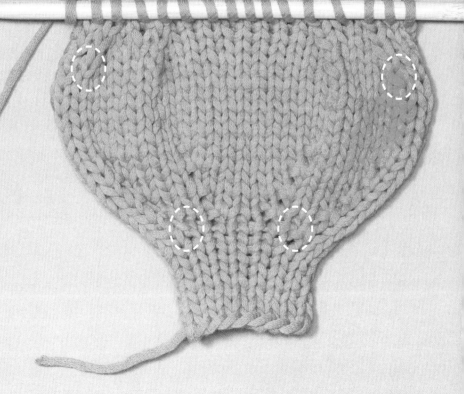

Row 33 K2, SKP, K4, K2tog, K2 (10 sts)
Row 34 P
Row 35 K
Row 36 P
Row 37 K
Row 38 P
Row 39 K
Row 40 P
Row 41 Cast off.

TOP PIECE – make one
Cast on 6 stitches in M using the large needles.
Row 1 K
Row 2 P
Row 3 K1, Kfb, K1 Kfb, K2 (8 sts)
Row 4 P
Row 5 K1, *Kfb* five times, K2 (13 sts)
Here you've got a lot of increasing, and the increase instructions within * are repeated. Written out fully, this row is: K1, Kfb, Kfb, Kfb, Kfb, Kfb, K2.

Row 6 P
Row 7 K1, *Kfb, K1* five times, K2 (18 sts)

There's more increasing again – this time the repeat is slightly different. Written out fully, it's: K1, Kfb, K1, Kfb, K1, Kfb, K1, Kfb, K1, Kfb, K1, K2.

Row 8 P
Row 9 K1, *Kfb, K2* five times, K2 (23 sts)
This is your final set of increases. You can work this one out!

Row 10 P
Work in St st until the piece measures 29cm (11½in) from the cast on edge, ending with a wrong side row.
St st is your other new abbreviation, which is short for stocking stitch. When a pattern has lots of rows knitted in stocking stitch it may give a measurement rather than listing every single row. You need to alternately knit and purl rows, working in St st until the piece measures 29cm (11½in) from the cast on edge. Ending with a wrong side row means ending after a purl row, so you when you work the last row

and turn the needle the right side will be facing towards you.

Reset your row counter back to 0.
Row 1 K2, SKP, K15, K2tog, K2 (21 sts)
Row 2 P
Row 3 K2, SKP, K13, K2tog, K2 (19 sts)
Row 4 P
Row 5 Cast off, leaving a long tail for sewing up.

FINS – make two
Cast on 8 stitches in M using the small needles.
This is where the needle size changes. If your tension was correct on 7mm (US 10½) needles use the 6mm (US 10) needles. If you had to adapt your needle size, you need to use the size smaller than the size that gave you the right tension.

Row 1 *K1, P1* all stitches
So far you've been knitting a row followed by purling a row, but now you're going to do both on the same

row. 'K1, P1' is short for 'knit one, purl one' and creates a ribbed fabric. You'll almost always see ribbed knitting on hats, jumpers, whale water bottle carriers and more. Rib stitch creates an elasticated, reversible fabric.

Here the pattern is asking you to *K1, P1* all stitches, so you need to knit a stitch, then purl a stitch, and repeat this sequence for the whole row. As you have 8 stitches on the row, written out fully it would be: K1, P1, K1, P1, K1, P1, K1, P1.

But wait! Before you start ribbing, go to page 68 for the full tutorial as there's something important you have to do with your yarn.

Row 2 *K1, P1* all stitches
Your second row is also *K1, P1* all stitches. With rib stitch you're always knitting over the knit stitches and purling over the purl stitches on the row (see below for some extra help).

Row 3 *K1, P1* all stitches
Row 4 *K1, P1* all stitches
Row 5 *K1, P1* all stitches
Row 6 *K1, P1* all stitches
Row 7 *K1, P1* all stitches
Row 8 *K1, P1* all stitches
Row 9 *K1, P1* all stitches
Row 10 *K1, P1* all stitches
Row 11 *K1, P1* all stitches
Row 12 *K1, P1* all stitches

Row 13 *K1, P1* all stitches
Row 14 *K1, P1* all stitches
Row 15 *K2tog* all stitches (4 sts)
Row 16 P
Row 17 K
Row 18 P
Row 19 Cast off, leaving a tail for weaving in.

STRAP – make one
Cast on 10 stitches in B using the small needles.
Row 1 *K1, P1* all stitches
Repeat Row 1 until the piece measures 120cm (47¼in) unstretched. It's important to measure it unstretched to make sure it will fit properly.
Next Row: Cast off, leaving a long tail for sewing up.

UNDER PIECE – make one
Cast on 6 stitches in C using the small needles.
Row 1 K
Row 2 P
Row 3 K1, Kfb, K1 Kfb, K2 (8 sts)
Row 4 P
Row 5 K1, *Kfb* five times, K2 (13 sts)
The under piece of the pattern uses the same increase as the top piece.

Row 6 P
Row 7 K1, *Kfb, K1* six times (19 sts)
Row 8 P
Row 9 K2* P1, K1* to the last stitch, K1
This is where the ribbing starts. So far you've been doing 'K1, P1' to create

the rib. You'll be continuing the action of moving the yarn backwards and forwards between the needles as you change from P to K, but there are knit stitches on either side of the rib. Follow the pattern and you'll see the rib stitch starting to form.

Row 10 P2, *K1, P1* to the last stitch, P1
This is where you'll notice the biggest difference with rib stitch. Unlike the fins and tail, this row starts with P2. After turning the needles ready to work Row 10, the first two stitches are bumpy, which means they're purls. Remember to purl over the purls and knit over the knits when ribbing.

Repeat Rows 9 and 10 until the piece on edge, ending on a wrong side (Row 10).
Next Row Cast off, leaving a long tail for sewing up.

SEWING UP
Weave in the loose ends on a fin piece. As there's no seam, weave them into the last two rows of the wrong side. When weaving in on reverse stocking stitch use the same instructions as garter stitch (see page 29). Just follow the smiles and frowns and trim the end. Repeat for the other fin.

Sew the top and under pieces together using mattress stitch (see page 75).

How to read your knitting: rib stitch

Rib stitch creates a stretchy fabric that is most commonly used on hats and garments. It has a reversible pattern with distinctive columns created by knit and purl. It doesn't curl, so is great for scarves (and whale fins). When ribbing, always knit over the smooth V stitches and purl over the bumpy stitches. Here you can see that the V rows have built on top of each other, as with stocking stitch, and the purl stitches look like bumpy bars between the V knit stitches.

Cast on tail

◥ Knit stitch
● Purl stitch

Rib stitch

Knit 1, purl 1

Whenever I mention that I knit to somebody who doesn't craft, they almost always reply saying 'K1, P1', with a fond memory of a family member whose needles used to click away while watching the TV. What they're referring to is 'knit 1, purl 1', which is most commonly used for rib stitch. This reversible fabric builds on columns of knit and purl stitches. The rows are repeats of 'K1, P1' or a similar variation. Here you'll be knitting over the knit stitches and purling over the purl stitches to create a ribbed fabric.

It can take a few rows to see the pattern in your work, but the most important thing to do is to always check that each row is correct – if you do it incorrectly, the pattern will change. You can see how my knitters got on with rib stitch on the next page if you need a hand.

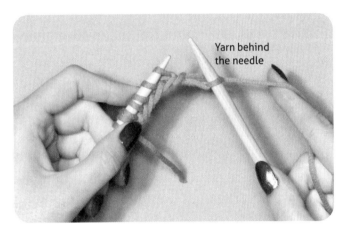

1. When a pattern asks you to *K1, P1* it's as simple as knitting a stitch followed by purling a stitch and repeating this pattern on the same row. Start by K1 (knit one stitch). As it's a knit stitch, the yarn will be behind the needle.

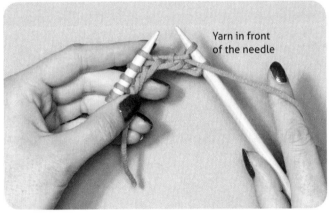

2. This is the important thing that I mentioned in the pattern. Move the yarn between the two needles, from the back to the front of the work, so that it's facing you. If you don't move it and purl, you'll create a new stitch.

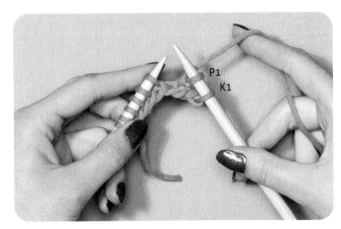

3. Once the yarn has moved and is facing you, P1 (purl one stitch). After you've purled, move the yarn between the needles so that it's at the back of the work.

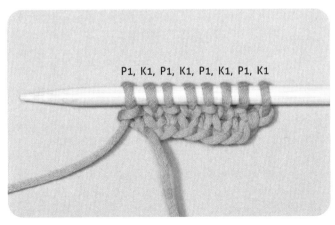

4. Work the rest of the row. K1, followed by P1, ensuring that you move the yarn to the back for Ks and to the front for Ps. Apply this every time K and P are worked on the same row.

Project 4 mistakes

A little bit of help

Learning purl is quite a big thing, especially with the whale project as you're using stocking stitch and rib. It's like learning anything for the first time and I was so proud to see how confident my knitters were with the knit stitch and how they took on purl. Here

are four mistakes that I documented while they were making the whale. With the first three projects we spent a lot of time at the studio but, like the tiger scarf, after the knitters got the hang of purl they finished the whale by themselves. This is the last catch

up page in the book as from here you've got the skills to make the other projects. If you get stuck in the future you can visit firsttimeknits.com. There's an FAQ section where you can tell me your mistakes and I'll be there to point you in the right direction.

On the above piece, after Row 10 it asks you to work in St st (stocking stitch). Amala thought this meant knit every row and worked in garter stitch. It's always a good idea to double check the abbreviations to make sure you're working the right stitch. Here she'll need to unravel the garter rows back.

On the above piece, after working the St st, it asks you to reset the row counter and work the last few rows. Zoë started Row 1 on the wrong side. St st tends to finish on a purl row, so the next row will be a knit row (Row 1). Zoë's last few rows are in reverse stocking stitch, so she'll need to unravel these.

Simon has knitted the strap piece in rib but not moved the yarn between the needles, which adds a new stitch. Always move the yarn backwards and forwards when working in rib, behind the needles for knit stitches and in front for purls.

This is a mistake I saw all of my knitters make – knitting the wrong stitches in the rib pattern. Rib stitch is formed by columns of knitting over the 'V's and purling over the bumps, but Katie has knitted over the purls and purled over the knits.

going back in time 2

There's always a sequel

When you were learning the knit stitch if you made a mistake you went back in time to fix it. You can do exactly the same when purling or working in stocking stitch. The original steps from page 23 will still apply to unravelling

any knit stitches. If you need to unravel a purl row stitch by stitch see Steps 1 and 2 on the next page. My knitters were confident at knitting and purling but would make the common mistake of knitting on a purl row or vice versa.

When this happens it may take a few rows to notice and then it can take ages to individually unravel all of the stitches. So, here's a handy way to go back in time with your stitches, and save time while doing so.

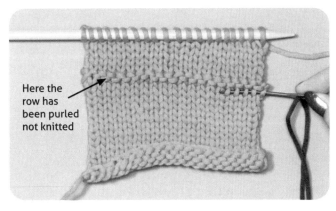

Here the row has been purled not knitted

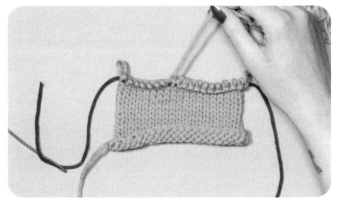

1. If you've made a mistake several rows back, there is another way to unravel the work. Thread a darning needle with some scrap yarn. On the right side of the work, find the row below the mistake and push the needle and yarn through the right loop of each V stitch on the row.

2. Once you've threaded the scrap yarn through all the stitches, it is safe to unravel. Take the work off the needle and pull the yarn until it reaches the loops on the scrap yarn. You won't be able to unravel them any further. This method saves time as you won't have to individually undo each stitch.

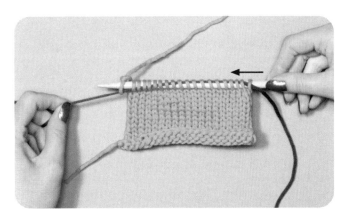

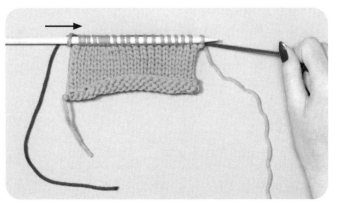

3. If you've unravelled the work and the yarn is on the left of the piece, push the needle from the right of the piece. You need to put the stitches back on the needle with the right part of the loop over the front of the needle. If the stitches twist you can fix them by following the tutorial on page 72.

4. If you've unravelled the work and the yarn is on the right of the piece, push the needle from the left of the piece. You need to put the stitches back on the needle with the right part of the loop over the front of the needle. If the stitches twist you can fix them by following the tutorial on page 72.

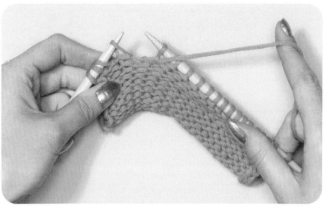

1. If you notice a mistake in the purl row that you're working on, unravel it stitch by stitch. As with undoing a knit stitch, start by placing the tip of the left needle into the front of the stitch below the first stitch on the right needle.

2. Move the right needle away and pull the yarn. This is the same action as unravelling a knit stitch, but with the yarn at the front of the work. If unravelling a rib row, move the yarn backwards and forwards between the work as you unravel.

Twisted stitches

Turn them around

It doesn't matter if it's a knit or a purl, your stitches should always sit on the needle with the right part of the loop coming over the front of the needle. The loops look so similar when they're all on the needle, but when you come to a twisted stitch you'll notice that something is not quite right. A twisted stitch will be facing the wrong way on the needle, with the left part of the loop coming over the front instead of the right. There are a number of reasons why your stitches may become twisted, like winding the yarn around the needles the wrong way. Also, if you unravel lots of rows you can easily put the stitches back onto the needle the wrong way, twisting them. If you were to knit or purl a twisted stitch it would show in the finished fabric, so it's best to fix them as soon as you spot one.

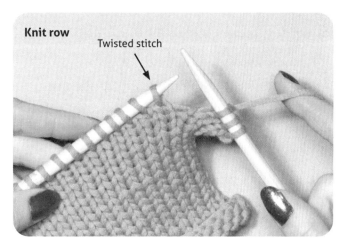

Knit row Twisted stitch

1. On a knit row, a twisted stitch will look like this. Notice how the stitch is facing a different way to all of the others. Don't worry – there's a simple fix.

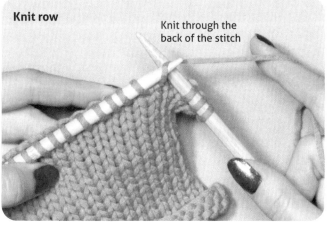

Knit row Knit through the back of the stitch

2. Instead of knitting through the front of the stitch as usual, knit into the back of it. This will turn the stitch the right way. Do this any time you find a twisted stitch on a knit row.

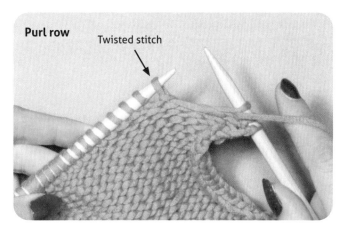

Purl row Twisted stitch

3. Here the stitch is twisted on a purl row, which is the wrong side of the work. The loop is facing the opposite way to all of the other stitches.

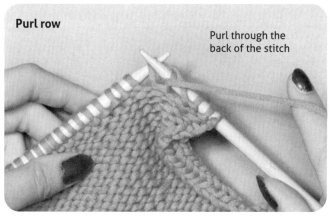

Purl row Purl through the back of the stitch

4. Push the right needle from the back to the front of the stitch and then purl it as usual to turn it the right way. Do this any time you find a twisted stitch on a purl row.

Dropped stitches 2

Pick them up

As purling is different to knitting, the mistakes and fixes change too. The same principles apply to similar mistakes, but the actions change. If you make a mistake on a knit row you can follow the fixing pages from Project 1. If you've dropped a stitch while working and the horizontal strand is at the front of the work you can pick it up using the tutorial from page 25. If you drop a stitch and the bar is behind the stitch that's dropped you'll need to pick it up using this method. The same general rules apply. For example, if a stitch drops off the needle and doesn't unravel just pop it back on. Or put a safety pin onto the dropped stitch to stop it from laddering down several rows. If this does happen there is a second advanced dropped stitch tutorial at firsttimeknits.com.

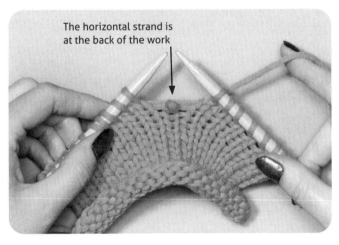

1. Here the stitch has dropped and unravelled on a purl row with the horizontal strand running along the back of it. It can be harder to see this as it's behind the dropped stitch.

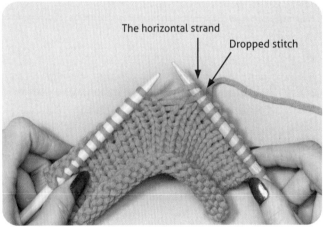

2. Use the right needle to pick up the dropped stitch, place the tip through the front of the dropped stitch and then under the horizontal strand behind it.

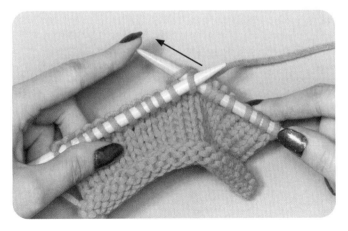

3. Put the left-hand needle tip into the back of the dropped stitch on the right needle, then lift the stitch over the strand and transfer it off the needle.

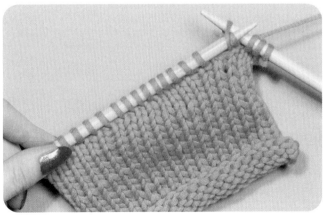

4. The rescued stitch will be on the right needle. Put the tip of the left needle through the front of the stitch and slip it over to the left needle, ready to be worked.

Incomplete stitches 2

When knitting in stocking stitch

When you were learning the knit stitch you might have stumbled across an occasional incomplete stitch. This may also happen when working in stocking stitch. As I've mentioned on the other fixing pages, the actions to correct a mistake are very similar, or even the same, as fixing garter stitch issues. An incomplete stitch on a knit or purl row will look like two weird stitches, and if you were to work both of them you'd add an extra stitch. Incomplete stitches occur when you wrap the yarn around the needle and don't bring it through the stitch. Here I've included how to fix incomplete stitches on a knit row (the right side) and on a purl row (which is the wrong side). If you come across an incomplete stitch, identify which side of the work you're on and follow the steps that apply to you.

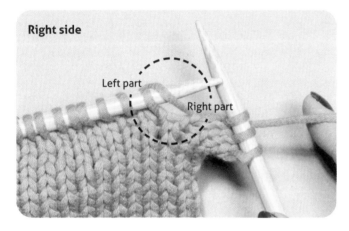

1. This incomplete stitch is in the middle of the row on the right side, which is a knit row. As in the first incomplete stitches tutorial (page 24), the stitch has two parts – the left and the right. Knit the row up to the incomplete stitch.

2. Take the right needle and place it through the back of the left part of the stitch. Lift the left part of the stitch over the right part, transfer it completely over the right part and off the needle. The stitch is now ready to be knitted as usual.

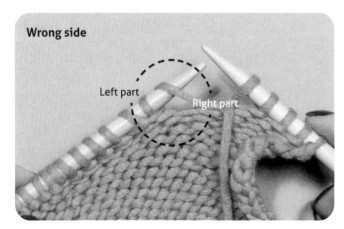

1. This incomplete stitch is in the middle of the row on the wrong side, which is a purl row. Again, the stitch has a left part and a right part. Purl the row up to the incomplete stitch.

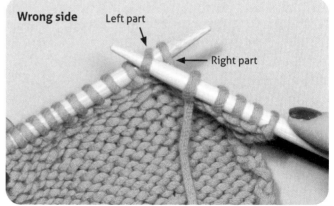

2. Place the right needle through the front of the left part, then lift and transfer it over the right part. The stitch is now ready to be purled as usual.

Mattress stitch

A magical sewing stitch

Mattress stitch is a lovely thing – it's a sewing stitch that creates an invisible seam. It is also known as a ladder stitch, which I think sums it up perfectly as it makes a zigzag stitch up the work that looks like a ladder. So far you've been using backstitch, which is great for sewing up garter stitch projects.

However, when knitting in stocking stitch, mattress stitch is the preferred sewing stitch. I absolutely love it and here I'll show you why.

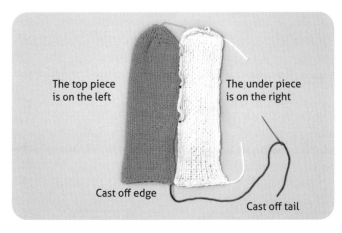

The top piece is on the left

The under piece is on the right

Cast off edge

Cast off tail

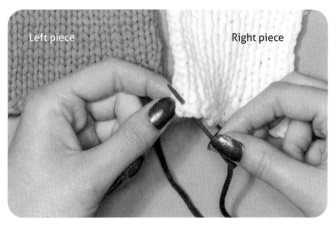

Left piece

Right piece

1. Place the top and under pieces next to each other, with the right sides facing up and the cast off edges (the widest parts) in line with each other. Pin one side of the pieces together from the cast off to the cast on edge to keep them in place. Thread the cast off tail of the top piece through a darning needle. I'm using a contrast colour here to demonstrate.

2. To secure these two pieces together you will need to make what's known as a 'figure of eight'. This is because once you've finished this sewing stitch it will look like a horizontal figure eight. On the right piece, push the needle and yarn from the back of the work through the middle of the first V stitch on the first row and out the other side.

3. Take the needle back to the left piece and push it through the first V stitch on the first row, from the back of the work and then out. Repeat Step 2, pushing it out of the first stitch on the first row of the right piece again. Pull the yarn to tighten it and the figure of eight will form).

4. Now it's time to start the mattress stitch. On the left side find the first two knit stitches closest to the edge and pull them apart – this will reveal bars that link the V stitches together. You'll be sewing into these bars, which will mean that you'll lose one stitch on the edge of the seam.

5. On the left piece, find the first bar that links the first and second V stitches together – it will be just above the cast on edge. Push the needle under and out of the bar.

6. On the right piece, pull the first and second knit stitches to find the bars between them. Push the needle under and out of the bar just above the cast on edge.

7. Move back to the left piece and find the bar above the bar you last sewed under. Push the needle under and out of this bar. Find the bar above the last bar you sewed through on the right piece, and sew under and out of it. The yarn will zigzag across the two pieces. Repeat this step several times.

8. After a few repeats you'll have created a zigzag ladder across the two pieces. Pull the yarn tightly and the join will appear seamless. Pulling too tightly will gather the work – if this happens just pull the pieces apart slightly and it will even the mattress stitch out.

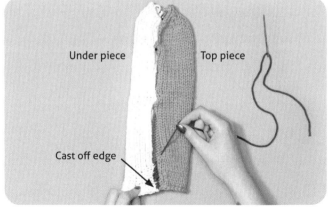

Under piece   Top piece

Cast off edge

9. Repeat Step 7 up to the last bars. Although the pieces change shape you will still find the bars between the first and second stitches at the edge of the pieces. End at the cast on edge but don't sew the cast on edges together. Weave the tail into the inside seam of the mattress stitch.

10. Fold the piece so that the open sides meet. The under piece will now be on the left and the top on the right. Use the under piece cast off tail or a new piece of M yarn to sew up using mattress stitch. Leave the cast on edges open and save the tail for later (see the sewing up tutorial on the next page).

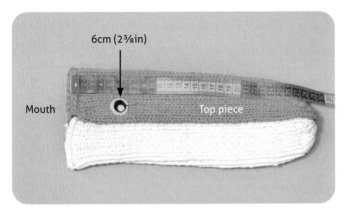

1. Lay the whale flat as shown. Cut out the eye templates from firsttimeknits.com in felt. On the top piece, place an eye 6cm (2⅜in) from the mouth and two V stitches above the seam. Sew the white sections onto the piece using backstitch with cotton thread. Be careful not to sew through both sides.

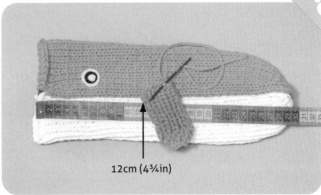

2. Place the cast on edge of a fin 12cm (4¾in) from the mouth along the sewing seam. Lay it slightly diagonally. Sew the cast on edge against the knit using M. Repeat Steps 1 and 2 on the other side of the whale, mirroring the instructions for the other eye and fin. Then turn the piece inside out.

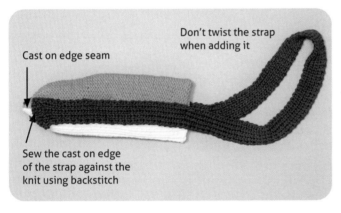

3. Sew up the open cast on edges using backstitch in M. Lay the strap flat across the piece, with the cast on edge above the cast on seam. Pin in place and sew up using backstitch in M, keeping the stitches small. Place the cast off edge of the strap on the other side of the piece and sew in place.

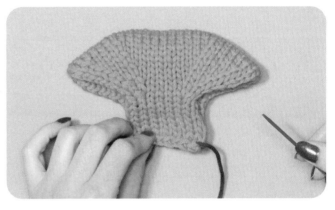

4. Turn the tail piece inside out so the right sides are facing up. Fold the tail in half so the cast on and off edges meet with the right sides facing up. Start with a figure of eight and sew along one side to the fold using mattress stitch in M. Sew up the other side in M. Leave the cast on and off edges open.

5. Place the tail at the end of the whale and pin in place. Pull the open end over the backstitches from the inside of the piece, hiding them. Sew through the edge of the tail into the knit of the whale on the top and under pieces. Then weave all the loose ends into the inside seam.

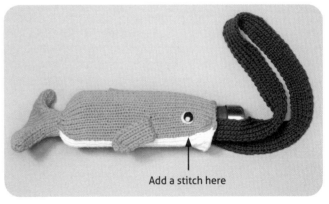

6. To secure the strap on the wrong side of the piece, measure 6cm (2⅜in) from the mouth and add a stitch through the inside seam and into the strap. Stitch several times to keep the strap in place. Repeat for the other side of the strap and weave the loose ends into the seam.

Finished projects

How did they get on?

After making the first three projects in quite a standard fibre I wanted to show you and the knitters that there are other yarns available that you might not expect to use when knitting. Yarn doesn't always have to be really woolly and warm – it can be smooth, soft and more summery. All of my knitters loved working with the cotton blend yarn! I was really impressed with them as they all took the whale home to work on once they'd got to grips with purling. There was the occasional unravelling, but overall, like the yarn, this project went really smoothly.

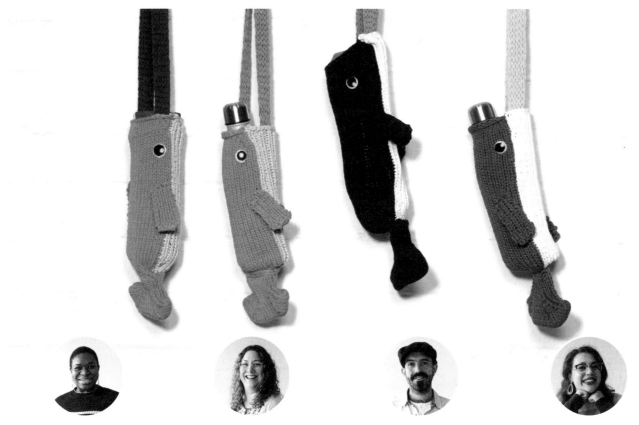

Amala: The whale yarn was lovely and stretchy and felt so nice. It was really quick to knit with. I just wanted to hug it! I made a couple of mistakes on the strap, but I noticed much later on and decided not to undo it as I don't think anybody would see them! I loved knitting the pieces but it took me a while to sew it up.

Katie: Learning the purl stitch was easier than I thought as I was nervous about trying it. I struggled with rib stitch at first but practice made perfect. By the middle of the strap I could chat and knit! I also learnt why measuring is important, as I had to re-sew my fin. I like mattress stitch and how neat it makes the seam.

Simon: The yarn was beautiful to work with and the range of patterns involved was really engaging. Once I got the hang of rib stitch I felt comfortable and enjoyed it. I made an Orca because it is my favourite mammal of the sea. I made the strap smaller so it would be more practical when I use it at festivals.

Zoë: I really loved working with this type of yarn. I found that I could knit quickly using it. I really liked purling, but it took me a while to get into the rib stitch. I had just bought a new water bottle, with a cute dark green theme so I wanted to make my whale to match it. The colours go perfectly together.

Project 5:
Turtle coaster

Texture, texture, texture

Now that you can knit, purl, increase and decrease, you can make almost any beginner pattern. So, for this project I'm not going to teach you a new stitch, instead you're going to use what you've already learnt but in a different way. My turtle coaster does have a new sewing technique though: the horizontal mattress stitch. Sounds intriguing, right?

Turtle coaster

MATERIALS

Scheepjes Stone Washed XL yarn (aran, 70% cotton/30% acrylic, 75m per 50g):

M (shell) – 1 ball
B (head and legs) – 1 ball
C (belly) – 1 ball

Scrap yarn for marking the stitches and black chunky yarn for the smile
Use some black yarn from the cup warmer.

Small needles: 4mm (US 6)
Large needles: 5mm (US 8)

Darning needle, handful of toy stuffing, 2 x 10mm (⅜in) toy eyes and washers
Here you need two new materials: toy eyes and stuffing. Both are easy to find online.

TENSION

14 stitches x 19 rows = 10cm (4in) in St st on 5mm (US 8) needles using C
Do I need to tell you again? Don't forget to swatch! Cast on 18 stitches and work 24 rows in C.

ABBREVIATIONS

K Knit
Kfb Knit into the front and back of the same stitch (increase)
K2tog Knit two stitches together (decrease)
... Repeat the instructions within the asterisks
P Purl
(sts) Stitches: The number of stitches you'll have at the end of the row
St st Stocking stitch: Knit a row, purl a row alternately

FINISHED SIZE: 13cm (5⅛in) wide x 19cm (7½in) long excluding legs

My turtle coaster uses the techniques you've already learnt in different ways. The legs use stocking stitch, and the shell and belly use variations of knit and purl to create different textures.

BACK LEGS – make two
Cast on 12 stitches in B using the large needles.
Row 1 K
Row 2 P all even rows.
Row 2 is different to the whale pattern as it's asking you to P all even rows. The good stuff happens on the odd rows and the even rows are purled.

Row 3 K
Row 5 K
Row 7 K
Row 9 *K2, K2tog* three times (9 sts)

Row 11 *K1, K2tog* three times (6 sts)
Row 12 P
I've included this P row to make sure you work it before the next row.

Cut the yarn, leaving a tail for sewing up. Thread it through a darning needle and push it through the remaining six stitches. Remove the needle (see image, below left). Pull the yarn tightly to gather the stitches. This will create a circle at the top of the piece.

Sew up the leg using mattress stitch with the yarn pulled tightly. Find the first bar on the right side of the leg, sew under and through it, then sew under and through the first bar on the left side. Repeat to the cast on edge, leaving the cast on edges open.

FRONT LEGS – make two
Cast on 16 stitches in B using the large needles.
Row 1 K
Row 2 P all even rows.
Row 3 K
Row 5 K
Row 7 K
Row 9 K
Row 11 K5, K2tog, K2, SKP, K5 (14 sts)
Row 13 K4, K2tog, K2, SKP, K4 (12 sts)
Row 15 K3, K2tog, K2, SKP, K3 (10 sts)
Row 17 K2, K2tog, K2, SKP, K2 (8 sts)
Row 19 K1, K2tog, K2, SKP, K1 (6 sts)
Row 20 P
I've included this P row to make sure you work it before the next row.

Cut the yarn, leaving a tail. Repeat the instructions for the back legs.

Thread the needle

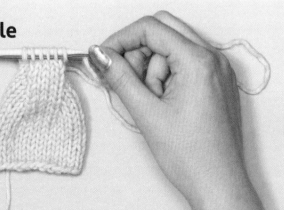

At the end of each leg cut the yarn and thread it through a darning needle. Then thread the needle through the remaining stitches and pull tightly.

Mark a stitch

Add scrap yarn or plastic markers to mark stitches. Don't tie the scrap yarn too tight though, as it'll need to be cut later.

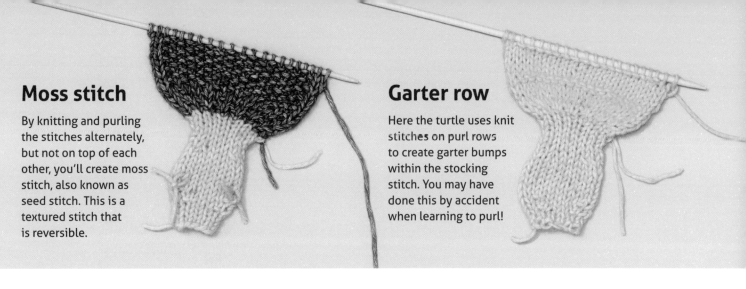

Moss stitch

By knitting and purling the stitches alternately, but not on top of each other, you'll create moss stitch, also known as seed stitch. This is a textured stitch that is reversible.

Garter row

Here the turtle uses knit stitches on purl rows to create garter bumps within the stocking stitch. You may have done this by accident when learning to purl!

TOP PIECE – make one
Cast on 7 stitches in B using the large needles.
Row 1 K
Row 2 P all even rows until stated.
Row 3 K
Row 5 K1, Kfb, K2, Kfb, K2 (9 sts)
Row 7 K1, Kfb, K4, Kfb, K2 (11 sts)
Row 9 K [adding a marker to the 3rd and 9th stitches]
Sometimes patterns use stitch markers – this helps when sewing up later. I like to tie a piece of scrap yarn to each stitch that needs marking, but you could also use plastic stitch markers (see image on previous page, right).

Row 11 K
Row 13 K
Row 15 K2, SKP, K3, K2tog, K2 (9 sts)
Row 17 K
Row 19 K
Row 21 Change to M, working all stitches in it from here on. K
Row 23 K1, *Kfb* six times, K2 (15 sts)
Row 25 K1, *Kfb, K1* six times, K2 (21 sts)
Row 26 P
I've included this P row to make sure you work it before the next row.

Reset your row counter back to 0.
Row 1 Change to the small needles. K2, *P1, K1* to the last stitch, K1
This row may look very familiar to you. That's because it's the same pattern used on the under piece of the whale. Work this row in exactly the same way.

As you're knitting and purling on the same row you need to go down a needle size, even if it's in the middle of a piece of knitting. Knit the stitches from the larger left needle to the smaller right one. Then use both smaller needles.

Row 2 P3, *K1, P1* to the last 2 stitches, P2
From here the even rows have been included. Your next instruction looks identical to rib stitch – essentially it is the same technique, but this time the K and P stitches are falling in different places, opposite to rib stitch. You'll be knitting on top of the P stitches and purling on top of the K stitches. This creates a distinctive stitch called moss stitch (see image, above left).

Rows 3–30 Repeat Rows 1 and 2.
Here the pattern is asking you to repeat the last two rows until Row 30.

Row 31 K2, K2tog, *P1, K2tog* five times, K2 (15 sts)
Row 32 P2, *K1, P1* to the last stitch, P1
Row 33 K3, *P1, K1* to the last 2 stitches, K2
Row 34 P2, *K1, P1* to the last stitch, P1
Row 35 K2, *K2tog* six times, K1 (9 sts)
Row 36 P
Row 37 K
Row 38 P
Row 39 Cast off loosely, leaving a tail for sewing up.

BELLY – make one
Cast on 7 stitches in B using the large needles.
Rows 1–26 Work from the top piece of the pattern.
As this part of the pattern is identical to the top piece, work Rows 1–26 from the top piece instructions, then return to the pattern for the next part.

Reset your row counter back to 0.
Row 1 K
<u>**Row 2**</u> P2, K17 P2
So far instructions for the even rows have been 'P all even rows', but this one has been <u>underlined</u> to show that it's worked differently. Here you need to purl 2, knit 17 and then purl 2.

Knitting on what's usually a P row will create a bumpy ridge like garter stitch (see image, above right). Continue purling all even rows until you reach the next <u>underlined</u> row.

Row 3 K
Row 5 K
Row 7 K
<u>**Row 8**</u> P2, K17 P2
Row 9 K
Row 11 K
Row 13 K
<u>**Row 14**</u> P2, K17 P2
Row 15 K
Row 17 K
Row 19 K
<u>**Row 20**</u> P2, K17 P2
Row 21 K
Row 23 K
Row 25 K
<u>**Row 26**</u> P2, K17 P2
Row 27 K
Row 29 K
Row 31 K1, *K1, K2tog* six times, K2 (15 sts)
Row 33 K
Row 35 K1, *K2tog* six times, K2 (9 sts)
Row 37 K
Row 39 Cast off loosely, leaving a tail for sewing up.

SEWING UP
See sewing up tutorial on page 83.

Horizontal mattress

Let's sew those horizontal seams together!

When sewing up a project using mattress stitch, the majority of the time you'll be using regular mattress stitch – the one I showed you on page 75. Regular mattress stitch is used to sew up the side of the work. However, when you need to sew cast on and off seams together you'll need to use horizontal mattress stitch. You can use backstitch, but this method is much easier and you'll save time as you won't have to turn the work inside out. Horizontal mattress stitch is sewn across the stitches and, like regular mattress stitch, creates neat seams.

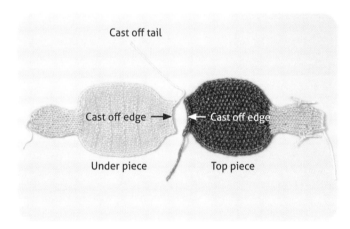

1. Place the cast off seams of the top and under pieces together with the right sides facing up. Thread the cast off tail from the under piece through a darning needle – we'll be using it to sew the cast off edges together. I'm using a contrast colour here to demonstrate.

2. Turn the pieces, so that the under piece cast off edge is above the top piece cast off edge. Push the needle and yarn through the under piece under the first stitch on the row below the cast off edge of the top piece. The needle needs to go under both parts of the V and out the other side.

3. Move the needle and yarn to the under piece, pushing them through the first stitch on the row above the cast off edge. Push them under both parts of the V and then out. This will zigzag the yarn between the two pieces.

4. Push the needle under both parts of the V stitch next to the first stitch that you sewed under on the top piece, then back up to the under piece and through the next V. Repeat several times to join the pieces. Pull tightly to secure.

1. Once you've sewn the cast off seam, sew up the sides using regular mattress stitch. Pin in place and apply the mattress stitch method from page 75 to the sides of the turtle, sewing between the bars to meet the cast on edges.

2. When you reach the cast on edge, sew the two cast on edges together using horizontal mattress stitch. Use the same technique as the cast off seams to join the pieces together. Pull the yarn tightly as you go.

3. Sew half way along the other side of the turtle using regular mattress stitch, leaving a gap at the end. Place the 10mm (⅜in) toy eyes over the stitch markers on the top piece and then turn inside out.

4. Push the washers over the eyes to secure them in place. If making the turtle for a child you should embroider the eyes instead, like you did for the cup warmer and tiger scarf. Turn inside out again. Stuff the head with polyester stuffing.

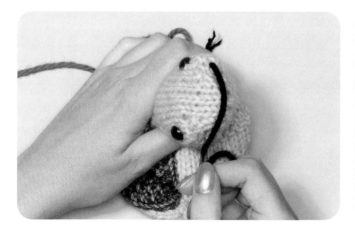

5. With black yarn, push the needle from the inside of the head, in line with an eye, out and across the seam and back into the seam, in line with the other eye. Weave the ends into the inside of the turtle. Sew up the gap using mattress stitch.

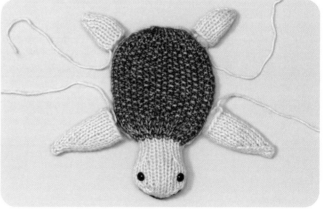

6. Stuff the legs. Place each front leg 2cm (¾in) from the neck as shown. Place the back legs at the end of the work, leaving a gap of 3cm (1⅛in) between them. Sew the cast on edges of the legs into the turtle using M. Push the ends in.

Finished projects

How did they get on?

After making the first four projects my knitters had all the skills to make their turtle coasters. Like with Project 3, a catch up section hasn't been included because any mistakes they made have been covered in the previous projects. I didn't see many issues with the turtles; the shells had a couple of odd stitches, but they've been hidden by the mugs. The finished turtles are all slightly different sizes as the knitters' tensions varied. A tip from my knitters is that if you haven't knitted for a while, make another swatch to ensure that the next piece you make will be the same size.

Amala: I love Terry the Turtle so much! I want to knit a whole family of turtles in different sizes. The stitches create lovely patterns. They look intricate but they were easier than I thought, because I'd learnt so much in the projects before. I chose the colours because I liked the contrast between the top and the bottom of the shell.

Katie: The underneath was fun to knit and great to see how using knit and purl makes different patterns. The horizontal sewing stitch was harder than the vertical one but, because I'd already done a type of mattress stitch, the new version quickly made sense. It was the first time I used stuffing and it was fun to see the turtle take shape.

Simon: I love the turtle! The variety of textures on the finished item and the proportions are great. The sewing together was a good challenge and it was an excellent way of practising the mattress stitch. I chose the colours because I thought the darker shell would be a nice contrast to the green and white.

Zoë: I found that my tension was a bit loose and my turtle is a bit bigger than the others. The sewing up was really tricky but I enjoyed the challenge! The end product was so cute though, so it's one of my favourites, for sure. I found this yarn really fun to work with and the colours reminded me of summer time.

You're a knitter now!

Congratulations! You're a knitter! My knitters can't believe that a short time ago they were learning to knit their phone cosies and now they can make whales, turtles, tigers and more. I'm often asked if my designs are hard to make and I always reply saying 'if you can knit, purl, increase and decrease you can make almost anything'. These are the four basic skills that most of my patterns are built on.

The next four projects focus on intermediate techniques. They take the skills you've learnt so far and introduce new things, like knitting seamlessly, loop stitch and colour change in the middle of a row. There's also the biggest project in the book, a jumper. As with some of the knits in the first five chapters, these projects do not include catch up pages – this is because most of the mistakes that you might make have been covered earlier, alongside how to fix them.

You can refer back to the fixing pages at any point. Plus, check out my knitters' reviews after each project for design inspiration and to see how they got on. Each intermediate project still has accompanying videos, and if you need any extra help there's always the FAQ section at firsttimeknits.com.

Project 6:
Burt the lion
Faux taxidermy at its finest

I started my career as a knitting pattern designer by making giant animal heads, so I knew I had to include one in this book. Meet Burt the lion – he's a kind fellow who is easier to make than you'd think. All you need to know is how to knit, purl, increase, decrease and make a loop stitch, which is what I'm going to teach you with this project.

Burt the lion

MATERIALS

Rico Creative Twist Super Chunky yarn (super chunky, 80% acrylic/20% alpaca, 75m per 100g):

M (main colour) – Yellow, 1 ball
B (loop colour) – Brown, 2 balls
C – Cream, 1 ball
D (nose) – Black, small amount

DK yarn in similar colour to B for sewing up

10mm (US 15) needles
200g (7oz) toy stuffing, heavy duty fishing line, stitch markers, darning needle, backing board, 2 x 24mm (1in) toy eyes and washers
Find backing board at firsttimeknits.com.

TENSION

9 stitches x 12 rows = 10cm (4in) in St st on 10mm (US 15) needles using M

ABBREVIATIONS

K Knit
Kfb Knit into the front and back of the same stitch (increase)
SKP Slip a stitch, knit a stitch and pass the slipped stitch over (decrease)
K2tog Knit two stitches together (decrease)
... Repeat the instructions within the asterisks
P Purl
L Loop stitch
(sts) Stitches: The number of stitches you'll have at the end of the row
Loop stitch is the new technique for this section.

FINISHED SIZE: 25cm (9⅞in) high x 19cm (7½in) wide x 33cm (13in) deep

---

This pattern features fewer annotations, but there will be a few along the way.

UNDER PIECE – make one
Cast on 8 stitches in C.
Row 1 K
Row 2 P all even rows.
Row 3 K1, *Kfb, K1* three times, K1 (11 sts)
Row 5 K1, *Kfb, K2* three times, K1 (14 sts)
Row 7 K
Row 9 K
Row 11 Change to M, working all stitches in it until otherwise stated. K. Add the yarn at the beginning of the row (see page 50). Cut the old yarn – you'll weave it in later.

Row 13 K3, Kfb, K2, Kfb, K2, Kfb, K4 (17 sts)
Row 15 K1, *Kfb, K4* three times, K1 (20 sts)
Row 17 K
Row 19 K
Row 21 K1, *Kfb, K5* three times, K1 (23 sts)
Row 23 K
Row 25 K
Row 27 K1, *Kfb, K6* three times, K1 (26 sts)
Row 29 K
Row 31 Change to B, working all stitches in it from here on. K

Row 33 K2, L22, K2
L stands for loop stitch. L is the abbreviation and the number indicates the number of times you need to work it. Head to page 89 for the tutorial.

Row 34 P
After the excitement of the loop row, don't forget to purl the even rows.

Row 35 K2, *L1, K1* to the last two stitches, K2
Loop stitch is used in a *L1, K1* repeat. Row 33 formed the start of the lion's mane, but here the pattern uses loop 1 and knit 1 alternately. K2 as usual, then follow the instructions within *, looping 1 and knitting 1 up to the last two stitches. Knit the last two stitches.

Row 37 K2, *K1, L1* to the last two stitches, K2
These loop and knit stitches alternate from the previous row. K2 as usual, then *K1, L1* to the last two stitches and K2.

Row 39 K2, *L1, K1* to the last 2 stitches, K2
Row 41 K2, *K1, L1* to the last 2 stitches, K2
Row 43 K2, *L1, K1* to the last 2 stitches, K2
Row 45 K2, *K1, L1* to the last 2 stitches, K2

Row 47 K2, *L1, K1* to the last 2 stitches, K2
Row 49 K
Row 51 Cast off loosely.
You need to cast off loosely to ensure that the piece fits on the backing board.

TOP PIECE – make one
Cast on 8 stitches in C.
Row 1 K
Row 2 P all even rows.
Row 3 K1, *Kfb, K1* three times, K1 (11 sts)
Row 5 K1, *Kfb, K2* three times, K1 (14 sts)
Row 7 K
Row 9 K
Row 11 Change to M working all stitches in it until otherwise stated. K
Row 13 K4, Kfb, K3, Kfb, K5 (16 sts)
Row 15 K4, Kfb, K5, Kfb, K5 (18 sts)
Row 17 K4, Kfb, K7, Kfb, K5 (20 sts)
Row 19 K
Row 21 K1, Kfb, K2, Kfb, K9, Kfb, K2, Kfb, K2 (24 sts)
Row 23 K [adding markers to the 7th and 17th stitches]
As with the turtle (see page 80), the lion also uses stitch markers. Add a marker to the 7th and 17th stitches.

Row 25 K2, Kfb, K3, Kfb, K9, Kfb, K3, Kfb, K3 (28 sts)
Row 27 K

Row 29 K8, Kfb, K9, Kfb, K9 (30 sts)
Row 31 Change to B, working all stitches in it from here on. K
Row 33 K2, L26, K2
Loop every time you see an L.

Row 35 K2, *L1, K1* to the last 2 stitches, K2
Row 37 K2, *K1, L1* to the last 2 stitches, K2
Row 39 K2, L1, K9, L1, K1, L1, K1, L1, K9, L1, K3
Row 41 K3, L1, K7, L1, K1, L1, K1, L1, K1, L1, K7, L1, K1, L1, K2
Row 43 K2, *L1, K1* to the last 2 stitches, K2
Row 45 K3, *L1, K1, L1, K1, K2tog* four times, K3 (26 sts)
Row 47 K2, L1, *K1, L1, K1, K2tog* four times, L1, K2 (22 sts)
Row 49 K
Row 51 Cast off loosely.

EARS – make two
Cast on 12 stitches in M.
Row 1 K
Row 2 P all even rows.
Row 3 K
Row 5 K
Row 7 K
Row 9 K
Row 11 K1, SKP, K1, SKP, K2tog, K1, K2tog, K1 (8 sts)
Row 13 K1, SKP, K2, K2tog, K1 (6 sts)
Row 15 K1, Kfb, K1, Kfb, K2 (8 sts)
Row 17 *K1, Kfb, Kfb* twice, K2 (12 sts)
Row 19 K
Row 21 K
Row 23 K
Row 25 K
Row 27 Cast off.

NOSE – make one
Cast on 3 stitches in D.
Row 1 K
Row 2 P all even rows.
Row 3 Kfb, Kfb, K1 (5 sts)
Row 5 Kfb, K2, Kfb, K1 (7 sts)
Row 7 Cast off.

SEWING UP
Unlike your previous projects there's not a full sewing tutorial here. Knitting patterns may only use written instructions, so following them is a good skill to have. Apply what you've already learnt. If you get stuck, there's a sewing up video at firsttimeknits.com.

Take the top and under piece (the top piece is the one with the markers) and place them together with the right sides facing up and the cream cast on edges together. Pin the edges in place and sew up using the horizontal mattress stitch technique (see page 82). Either use the cast on tail or use a new piece of C yarn.

Pin one of the sides together, from the sewn up cast on edge to the cast off edge. The colour changes on both pieces need to meet as you pin. Leave the cast off edges unpinned. Tuck the loose tails inside the piece to weave in later. Sew up from the cast on edge to the C and M colour change using mattress stitch (see page 75) in C. Sew under two bars at a time to make the mattress stitch quicker. Remove the pins as you sew up. Weave the C yarn into the inside seam. Then sew to the M and B colour change using mattress stitch in M. Sew the B section together using mattress stitch in

B. Weave the loose ends into the inside seam. Mirror the instructions for the other side of the head. Do not sew the cast off edges together.

Place the cast off edge of the nose (the widest part) in the centre of the top piece, over the C and M colour change. Sew in place using D. Sew a small line in D from the bottom of the nose down to the cast on edge seam. Weave the D tails into the inside of the piece. Place the eyes over the markers. Remove the markers and secure with washers on the wrong side of the piece. If making for a child, embroider the eyes instead.

Fold an ear in half so that the cast on and cast off edges meet. Sew up to the fold using mattress stitch in M. Repeat for the other side, leaving the cast on and cast off edges open, then stuff the ear. Repeat for the second ear. Find the bald areas in the B section of the top piece (where there are no loops) and place each ear horizontally in these bald areas. Sew the ears onto the head in M, mimicking the horizontal mattress stitch by sewing under and out of the stitches on the first row of the ears, then under and out of the stitches below them on the head. Sew the edges of the ears onto the head, leaving them slightly open so that they stand up straight. Weave in all the loose ends on the wrong side.

Stuff, following the shape of the head. The cast off edges will be open with the stuffing exposed. Sew on the backing board. As this is a new technique I've included a tutorial on page 90.

Loop stitch

Every time you L it will create a big loop on the piece. The stitches are pretty easy to count as one loop equals one L stitch. At the top of the loop stitch you'll see the slipped part of the stitch, which leans to the left. On the back of the piece the loop stitches will look a little uglier and bigger than usual, almost like a crochet stitch. That's completely normal and nobody is going to see them!

Loop stitch

The perfect stitch for a curly blow dry

I always think of loop stitch as the child of Kfb and rib, as it uses steps from both stitches. The loop stitch is great for adding volume and texture to your knit, as with the lion's mane. This stitch can feel like you have to put in a lot of work, but once you get into the rhythm of working the loop, it can be really fun. The loop stitch used on the lion has an approximate length of 13cm (5⅛in), but loop stitches in other patterns will vary. I tend to measure my first couple of loop stitches, then base the row on those. If the loops are slightly bigger or smaller I think they look more natural.

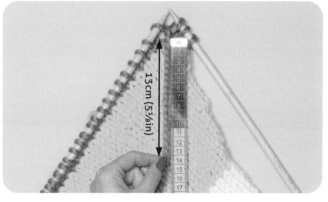

1. The first instruction in the pattern is to K2, so knit the first two stitches as usual and then apply the loop stitch to the next stitch. It starts in the same way as a Kfb: knit into the front of the stitch, transferring the new stitch onto the right needle, but don't knit into the back of the stitch.

2. Leave the needles as they are, with the half-made stitch still on the right needle. As with rib stitch, move the yarn from the back of the work and between the two needles. Then lay it down the front of the work. Measure approximately 13cm (5⅛in) of the yarn down the work.

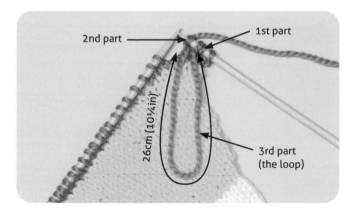

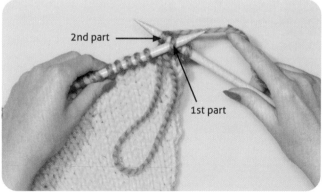

3. Loop the yarn another 13cm (5⅛in) back to the needles and move it between them – you'll have measured 26cm (10¼in) in total. As with Kfb, knit into the back of the stitch. As you've Kfb-ed, an extra stitch has been added. The L stitch is made up of three parts: the K into the front (1st part), the K into the back of the stitch (2nd part) and the loop (3rd part).

4. You need to decrease the extra stitch – you can do this like an SKP. Slip the 1st part of the loop stitch over the 2nd part and off the needle to secure the loop. On the back of the work the loop stitch will look uglier than usual. Use these steps every time you need to make a loop stitch. For Row 33 you need to L22, then K2, so you'll get lots of practice.

1. Once the head is stuffed, place the backing board inside it with the arrow on the board facing up. Thread a darning needle with the colour B DK yarn, tie a large knot at the end and push it through the centre top hole and 2.5cm (1in) into the head. I've used a contrast colour here to demonstrate.

2. Pull the needle out, turn it around and sew back into the piece, close to where it exited. Sew through the knit and out of the cast off edge. Push the needle back through the centre top hole and 2.5cm (1in) out of the knit. Turn the needle around and sew back through the cast off edge.

3. From the cast off edge, move the needle anti-clockwise to the next hole on the board. Push the needle through the front of the hole and 2.5cm (1in) out of the head. Turn the needle around, as in Step 2, and sew it back out of the cast off edge. Pull the yarn as you do this to secure it.

4. Push the needle into the hole directly below where it just exited and 2.5cm (1in) into the back of the head. Again, following the technique from Step 2, turn the needle around and push it back into the head, close to where it exited, and then through the cast off edge.

5. Repeat Steps 3 and 4 around the board, leaving a quarter unsewn. If the piece feels like it needs additional stuffing, add it now. If you run out of yarn, add a new piece by tying a knot at the end and pushing it through the hole, as in Step 1. Sew up the remaining quarter.

6. Once you've sewn the board anti-clockwise repeat the process, mirroring Steps 3 and 4 clockwise. Thread the fishing line through the centre top hole, make a loop and tie using a secure reef knot. I've used a contrast colour to demonstrate. Hang the fishing line loop onto a nail in the wall.

Finished projects

How did they get on?

The last four projects in the book are beginner to intermediate level. As they all build on the skills that you learnt in the first part of the book, I haven't included any catch up pages.

My knitters did make a few mistakes here and there, but when they did I saw them unravelling the work, fixing the mistakes and then re-knitting the pieces. I gave the occasional helping hand – if you need one too, head to the FAQ section at firsttimeknits.com. All my knitters made different lions and it was lovely to see them hanging next to each other at SL HQ.

Amala: I love the loops! They were less complicated to knit than I thought they'd be and, once I got into it, I didn't want to stop looping. For this knit it was lovely to use bigger needles, because you get so much more done without realising it. After I sewed the lion together and stuffed it, it was great to see it all take shape.

Katie: I chose these colours because I wanted my lion to be bright. I thought the ears were really fun to make because you increase and decrease equally. I found that every so often I had to measure my loops, as I kept going rogue and they were uneven. Sewing onto the backing board took a while to get the hang of too.

Simon: The lion has been my favourite thing to knit out of all of the projects so far. I found the loop stitch tricky at first but once I understood the technique it was a very natural stitch to use. I adore the texture that the loop stitch creates on the lion's mane. I chose to make mine an albino lion because they are very rare.

Zoë: I thought the loop stitch would be hard but I found it really therapeutic. As my knitting is loose I swatched on 9mm needles and got my tension right! Aslan was my inspiration when putting this together because I love the Narnia books. It was quite hard sewing it to the board, but is so amazing and rewarding once it's done!

Project 7:
Bobble hat

Introducing circular knitting

I absolutely love a bobble hat and I've lost count of the number that I've made! I like how the colour combinations in hats give a glimpse of your personality. This project introduces circular knitting, which means you'll be working in the round, making a hat without a seam. Looking for baby sizes? Find my bonus patterns at firsttimeknits.com.

Bobble hat

MATERIALS

Sincerely Louise How Does It Feel yarn (chunky, 100% wool, 115m per 100g): This is my own brand of yarn, but I've also listed alternatives at firsttimeknits.com.

SMALL AND MEDIUM: M (main colour) – 1 ball
LARGE: M (main colour) – 2 balls
ALL SIZES: C (contrast colour) – 1 ball

Small needles: 5mm (US 8) circular needles with a 60cm (24in) cable
Large needles: 6mm (US 10) circular needles with a 60cm (24in) cable
DPNs: 6mm (US 10) 30cm (12in) DPNs
You need two new types of needles: circular and DPNs. DPNs are double-pointed needles – find them online or at most hobby shops.

TENSION

16 stitches x 20 rows = 10cm (4in) in St st on 6mm (US 10) needles
When working in the round you need to create a swatch where every row is a knit row. You still cast on 4 more stitches and work 4 more rows, making a 20 stitches x 24 rows square. Before making your swatch see page 96.

ABBREVIATIONS

K Knit
P Purl
K2tog Knit two stitches together (decrease)
DPNs Double-pointed needles
... Repeat the instructions within the asterisks
(sts) Stitches: The number of stitches you'll have at the end of the row

FINISHED SIZES: ADULT SMALL 52.5cm (20⅝in) circumference, MEDIUM 56cm (22in) circumference, LARGE 60cm (24in) circumference
Garment patterns often have all of the sizes written alongside each other. I've colour coded them to help when following the pattern.

It's time to learn something new! Go to page 94 for your first task, the long tail cast on, followed by a tension swatch.

ALL SIZES

Cast on 84, 90, 96 stitches in M using the small circular needles and the long tail cast on method. You'll need 300cm (118in) of yarn for the long tail.
See page 97 for the circular needles tutorial.

The long tail cast on creates the first round of knitting so this pattern will begin from Round 2 after the marker. **This pattern uses rounds instead of rows as it's worked in the round.**

Round 2 *K1, P1* all stitches
See Step 3 on page 97 for some help.

Repeat Round 2 until the rib measures **9.5cm, 10cm, 10.5cm (3¾in, 4in, 4⅛in)** from the cast on edge.
Next round Change to the large circular needles and C, then K all stitches.
See Step 5 on page 98.

Following rounds K all rounds until the piece measures **19cm, 20cm, 21cm (7½in, 8in, 8¼in)** from the cast on edge.

There's no purling after the rib! That's because stocking stitch is created by knitting over the knit stitches. Finish the last round at the stitch marker.

Reset the row counter. Here the pattern splits into sizes. For the **ADULT SMALL** follow **ALL SIZES**.

ADULT LARGE

Round 1 *K6, K2tog* twelve times (84 sts)
Round 2 K
Reset the row counter and work from the **ALL SIZES** pattern.

ADULT MEDIUM

Round 1 *K13, K2tog* six times (84 sts)
Round 2 K
Reset the row counter and work from the **ALL SIZES** pattern.

ALL SIZES

Round 1 *K5, K2tog* twelve times (72 sts)
Round 2 Switch to DPNs and K.
After this round the stitches on the needle will become harder to move, so it's time to switch to DPNs. See Step 7 on page 98.

After changing to DPNs each needle will have 24 stitches on it.
Round 3 *K4, K2tog* twelve times (60 sts, the split is 20, 20, 20)
I've included the stitch count and the split on each DPN.

Round 4 K
Every other round is a K – this accounts for what would usually be a purl row.

Round 5 *K3, K2tog* twelve times (48 sts, the split is 16, 16, 16)
Round 6 K
Round 7 *K2, K2tog* twelve times (36 sts, the split is 12, 12, 12)
Round 8 K
Round 9 *K1, K2tog* twelve times (24 sts, the split is 8, 8, 8)
Round 10 K
Round 11 *K2tog* twelve times (12 sts, the split is 4, 4, 4)
Round 12 K. Cut the yarn, leaving a tail.

Thread the tail onto a darning needle. Thread it through the remaining 12 stitches and pull tightly. Weave in the loose end on the wrong side. Fold the ribbed brim in half and sew on an 8cm (3in) pompom. Use a pompom maker or watch my easy pompom video online.

Long tail cast on

My favourite cast on

Your first task of Project 7 is to make your tension swatch using the long tail cast on. When you first learnt to knit all those pages ago I mentioned that there were other ways of casting on. The two needle cast on is great for beginners, but I'm going to take you to the next level with this technique. This cast on gives an elasticated edge and creates the first row of knitting, which is a bonus. It's called the long tail cast on because you have to judge the amount of yarn you need before you start and then you use that tail of yarn when casting on. I've worked out how much you need for this project, but for future knits you can find a calculation method at firsttimeknits.com.

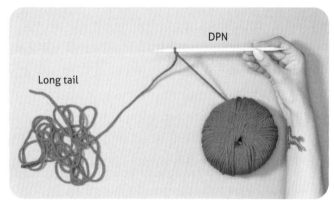

1. For this task you'll need one of your 6mm (US 10) DPNs. DPNs are double-pointed needles. Measure 70cm (28in) of the yarn (let's call it the long tail) and place it in a pile to the left of you. Make a slip knot from the yarn coming from the ball, not the tail, and place it on the left side of the DPN.

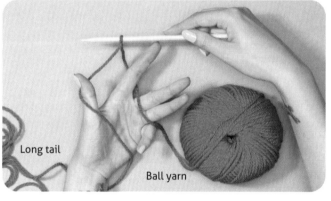

2. Hold the DPN in your right hand. Separate the two yarns coming from the slip knot. Move your left hand into an almost Vulcan salute. Run the yarn coming from the ball through your index and middle fingers and above your little finger. Run the yarn coming from the tail over your thumb.

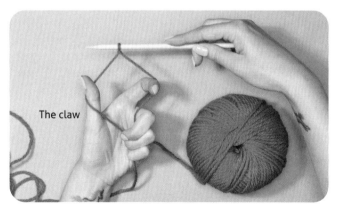

3. I like to call this next hand position 'the claw'. Bend your index finger so that the yarn from the ball runs over it. Close your three fingers to the palm of your hand, running both strands of yarn through them. The yarn from the ball will exit between your ring and little finger.

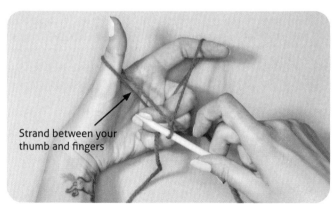

4. Pull the needle down and away from your claw hand, allowing both strands of yarn to run through the palm of your hand. Point the needle so that it is facing towards your thumb. Look at the yarn running around your thumb to your fingers – that's important.

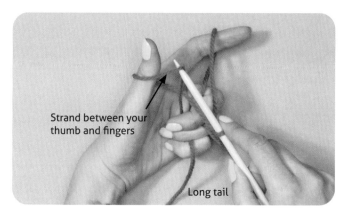

5. You now need to catch that strand of yarn running around your thumb to your three fingers – not the strand between your thumb and the needle. Move the needle under the strand and start moving it towards the right. You'll feel the long tail yarn that is under your fingers starting to move.

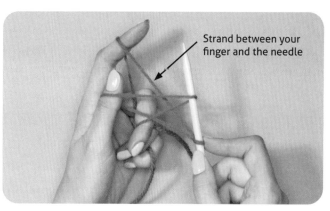

6. Continue moving the needle and the strand of yarn to the right, so they cross the other strand of yarn that is running between your index finger and the slip knot on the needle. By doing this a star shape will form. Take notice of the strand running between your index finger and the needle.

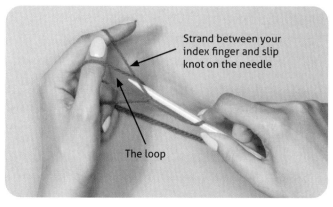

7. Move the needle tip under the strand running between your index finger and the slip knot on the needle, catching the strand. Move the needle under and towards you, through the loop in the centre of the star that is being held by your thumb. The star will lose its shape as you do this.

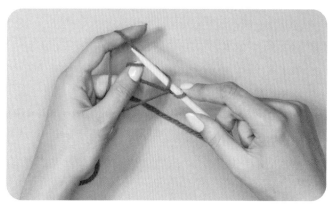

8. This is how the needle will look once you've moved it under the strand and through the centre of the star. Doing this adds a new loop to the needle – the loop will be sitting on your thumb as well as the needle. This is how you add a new stitch with the long tail cast on.

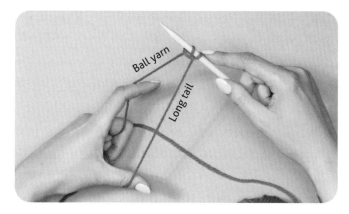

9. Keeping both yarns in your three fingers, remove your thumb from the loop and move it towards you, pushing it against the long tail. Move your thumb down to tighten the stitch onto the needle. Don't pull it too tight – as with the two needle cast on, let the stitch sit naturally on the needle.

10. Don't release the yarns from your hand; instead move back into the claw position from Steps 2 and 3. Pull the needle so that it faces your thumb. Repeat Steps 5–10 to cast on. For your swatch cast 20 stitches onto the DPN. Then see the next page for your tension task.

Tension in the round

Yes, it's another tension task

When working in the round you'll be knitting in a continuous circle. Before you start knitting your hat you need to make a tension square. This is really important because when working in the round your tension can change dramatically. This is due to the fact that most of the rows are knit stitches, which are looser than purl. To check your tension on circular needles you'd have to cast on enough stitches to fill the needles, which is around the amount of the hat, and knit 24 rows. This would be a waste of time. Instead you can use this cheeky method.

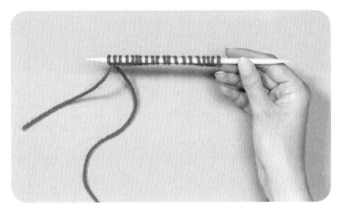

1. Once you've mastered the long tail cast on and have 20 stitches on your needle it's tension square time. For this task you'll need two of the 6mm (US 10) DPNs. These come in packs of 5 and you normally use them all – I'll explain how later. Leave the other 3 in the pack for this task.

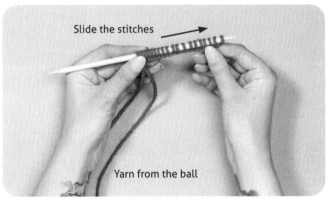

Slide the stitches

Yarn from the ball

2. You need to check your tension by knitting every row. You won't be purling at all. As the long tail cast on creates the first row, the yarn coming from the ball will be on the left of the needle as if it was ready to turn and purl. Instead of turning, slide all stitches to the right side of the DPN.

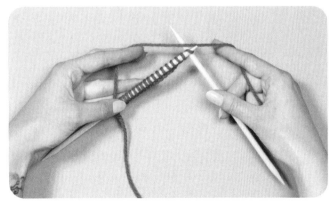

3. You now need to knit this row, but the yarn is still on the left side of the needle. Here's the solution: move the yarn across the back of the row – don't pull it at all, instead leave it super loose. Then start knitting with it. The first stitch will feel weird to knit. I must say, this is not how to use DPNs. The only time you'll work like this is to make your swatch!

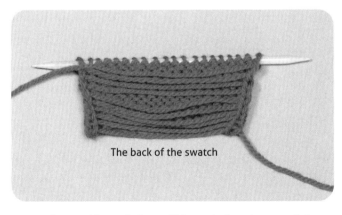

The back of the swatch

4. Your first and last stitches will be ugly, but the swatch has more stitches than you need so it doesn't matter. Repeat Steps 2–3, sliding the stitches and knitting every row, until you've worked 24 rows. The back of the swatch will have strands running across it and the front will be in stocking stitch. Measure as usual and adjust the needle size if required.

Circular knitting

Get around, round, round, I get around

As I mentioned before, working in the round means knitting in a continuous circle. You can either use a set of circular needles, DPNs or a mix of both, which is what you'll be doing here.

When making a hat you're essentially knitting a tube that decreases at the top. You'll be using a set of 5mm and 6mm (US 8 and 10) needles with a 60cm (24in) cable. The 60cm (24in)

measurement refers to the cable length between the two needles. Cables come in different lengths, but this size is perfect for your hat. Later you'll be switching to 6mm (US 10) DPNs.

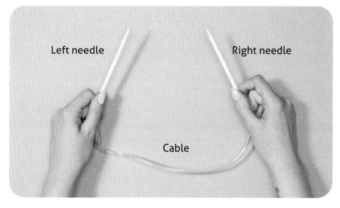

1. To start your hat, you'll need the small circular needles. The first part is worked in rib stitch and you always go down a size when working in rib. If your tension was correct on 6mm (US 10) needles, use 5mm (US 8) needles. These look odd, but they're just a pair of needles with a cable in the middle.

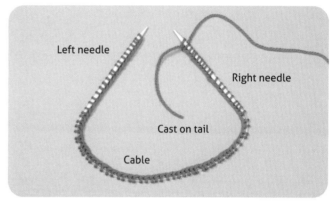

2. Measure 300cm (118in) of yarn and, using the right needle, cast on **84, 90, 96** stitches with the long tail cast on. Spread the stitches along the cable to the left needle. The most important thing is to make sure the cast on edge is not twisted. The stitches should all be flat and facing each other.

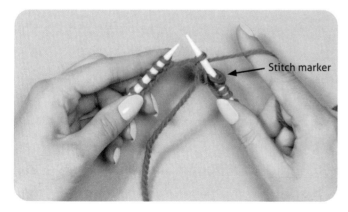

3. Add a stitch marker to the right needle – this marks the start of the row. As the long tail cast on creates the first round of knitting, the pattern begins at Round 2. This is: *K1, P1* all stitches. Knit the first stitch from the left to the right needle. Pull it tight as this will prevent a gap forming between the first and last stitches.

4. You've just knitted one, so now you need to purl one. Repeat *K1, P1* across the round. Your last stitch before the marker will be a P1. Once you've worked a round, the stitches will become easier to move around the needle. You'll be constantly sliding the stitches along the cable from the left to right needle – that's why it's called working in the round.

5. Work the *K1, P1* rib until the piece measures **9.5cm**, **10cm**, **10.5cm** (**3¾in**, **4in**, **4⅛in**) from the cast on edge. The next round is: Change to the larger needles and C, then K all stitches. Pull the right needle out of the work, pushing all the stitches along the cable to the left needle.

6. Tie the M yarn as usual. To change needle size, knit all the stitches from the small left needle to the large right needle. The next instruction is: K all rounds until the piece measures **19cm**, **20cm**, **21cm** (**7½in**, **8in**, **8¼in**) from the cast on edge.

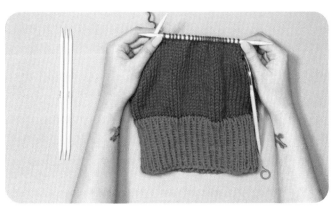

7. Follow the pattern to Round 2 of ALL SIZES. As you decrease you'll need to switch to DPNs. DPNs come in a pack of five, but you'll only need four. As in Step 5, pull the right needle away from the work. Remove the stitch marker for now. Knit the stitches from the cable needle to the DPN.

8. You'll be using three DPNs to hold the stitches. You need to work out the stitch split on the DPNs by dividing the number of stitches (72 sts) by three. Knit 24 stitches onto the first DPN, knitting the first stitch tighter than usual. Bunch up the stitches in the centre of the DPN to prevent them falling off.

9. Place the second DPN between the two needles. Knit the next 24 stitches onto it, ensuring that you pull the first stitch tighter than usual. This prevents the stitches between the needles being too loose. Bunch the stitches in the middle of the DPN. Repeat this step for the third needle.

10. The 4th needle is the working needle. Round 3 is: *K4, K2tog* twelve times, so repeat this across the DPNs. Put the marker between the first two stitches on the first DPN. As you knit one set of stitches to the working DPN, the empty DPN becomes the working needle. Repeat for the rest of the hat.

Finished projects

How did they get on?

My knitters have just made their first project on circular needles. I was on hand as they learnt the long tail cast on. I'd really recommend using the video tutorial when you learn it, as it's one of the trickiest techniques in the book. Saying that, Zoë picked it up so quickly and naturally! Once my knitters had the hang of the circular needles they were away! We saw a couple of issues on the first few rounds of rib, with Simon starting his again. Sometimes it can be easier to pull something apart and start again, rather than unravelling back to the beginning.

Amala: The circular needles were a bit daunting at first, but once I got used to them I loved knitting round and round and round. The DPNs didn't make sense at all when I first looked at them – I couldn't work out how I could knit with them. They were a bit fiddly, so maximum concentration was needed, but it was worth it!

Katie: After working on the whale, the rib stitch was easier to grasp on the new type of needle. The circular needles felt weird at first but I got used to them after a few rounds and by the end I loved using them. I was worried about trying the DPNs as I thought I might lose stitches, but they were easier than I expected!

Simon: I found working in the round the most difficult technique so far. I made mistakes early on in the knit, especially on the rib section, and had to start again. I actually preferred working on the DPNs as they felt more natural. I decided not to add a pompom to make the hat more practical as I wear hooded tops.

Zoë: It was tricky changing to DPNs and knitting in the round was definitely a challenge. Overall I loved learning this new technique, but it took me a while to warm up to it. I love combining blue and yellow, so putting this hat together was so aesthetically pleasing. It definitely knitted up faster than I thought.

Project 8:
Hot dog dog

Can I have fries with that?

I absolutely love designing fun knits and my hot dog dog has to be up there with the best of them. The dog is made from knit and purl, with a little bit of shaping. The mustard is created by changing in the middle of the work and the buns were freshly prepared this morning! You can also upgrade your order using super chunky yarn.

SKILL LEVEL INTERMEDIATE

Hot dog dog

MATERIALS

Stylecraft Special DK yarn
(DK, 100% acrylic, 144m per 100g):
M (main colour) – Walnut, 1 ball
B – Camel, 1 ball
C – Cream, 1 ball
D – Sunshine, 1 ball

This project was designed in DK yarn, which is a lighter weight and uses smaller needles. However, as it's a toy you can choose which size needles and yarn to make it with. You could make it bigger by using a chunkier yarn! Head to the Project 8 section at firsttimeknits.com for my shopping lists and see my knitters' hot dog dogs on page 105.

4mm (US 6) needles

50g (1¾oz) toy stuffing, darning needle, 2 x 8mm (⅜in) toy eyes and washers for the eyes, 1 x 10mm (½in) toy eye and washer for the nose

TENSION

22 stitches x 30 rows = 10cm (4in) in St st on 4mm (US 6) needles using D
If making in another yarn, use the recommended tension on the ball band.

ABBREVIATIONS

K Knit
Kfb Knit into the front and back of the same stitch (increase)
SKP Slip a stitch, knit a stitch and pass the slipped stitch over (decrease)
St st Stocking stitch: Knit a row, purl a row alternately
K2tog Knit two stitches together (decrease)
... Repeat the instructions within the asterisks
P Purl
sts Stitches: The number of stitches you'll have at the end of the row

FINISHED SIZE: 26cm (10¼in) long excluding tail x 14cm (5½in) wide

YARN MARKERS

This project uses various coloured markers, which are referenced when sewing up. Keep a note of which colour you've used for each letter.

Colour U – Left leg   **Colour V** – Right leg   **Colour W** – Eyes
Colour X – Left ear   **Colour Y** – Right ear

This project introduces a new colourwork technique on the top piece. Work the other plain pieces first.
I recommend using long tail cast on (see page 94), as it creates the first row, but you can use the two needle cast on (see page 12) and knit the first row. Each part of the pattern begins from Row 2.

UNDER PIECE – make one
Cast on 5 stitches in M.
Row 2 P all even rows.
Row 3 K1, *Kfb* three times, K1 (8 sts)
Row 5 K1, *Kfb, K1* three times, K1 (11 sts)
Row 7 K
Row 9 K
Row 11 K
Row 13 K
Row 15 K
Row 17 K1, *Kfb, K2* three times, K1 (14 sts)
Row 19 K
Row 21 K1, *Kfb, K3* three times, K1 (17 sts)
Row 23 K1, *Kfb, K4* three times, K1 (20 sts)
Row 25 K

Row 27 K
Row 29 K
Row 31 K
Row 33 K [adding colour U markers to the 5th and 9th stitches and colour V markers to the 12th and 16th stitches]
Row 35 K
Row 37 K
Row 39 K [adding colour U markers to the 5th and 9th stitches and colour V markers to the 12th and 16th stitches]
Rows 41–64 Work in St st
Make sure you purl Row 40 before you start working in St st. Row 41 is a K row. The St st ends with a P row at Row 64.

Row 65 K [adding colour U markers to the 5th and 9th stitches and colour V markers to the 12th and 16th stitches]
Row 67 K
Row 69 K
Row 71 K [adding colour U markers to the 5th and 9th stitches and colour V markers to the 12th and 16th stitches]
Row 73 K
Row 75 K
Row 77 K1, *K1, K2tog* six times, K1 (14 sts)

Row 79 K1, *K2tog* six times, K1 (8 sts)
Row 81 K1, SKP, K2, K2tog, K1 (6 sts)
Row 83 Cast off.

EARS – make four
Cast on 5 stitches in M.
Row 2 P all even rows.
Row 3 K1, *Kfb* three times, K1 (8 sts)
Row 5 K
Row 7 K1, *Kfb, K1* three times, K1 (11 sts)
Row 9 K
Row 11 K
Row 13 K
Row 15 K
Row 17 K2, SKP, K3, K2tog, K2 (9 sts)
Row 19 K2, SKP, K1, K2tog, K2 (7 sts)
Row 21 Cast off.

LEGS – make four
Cast on 14 stitches in M.
Row 2 P
Rows 3–14 Work in St st
Row 15 K1, *K2tog* six times, K1 (8 sts)
Row 16 P
Cut the yarn, leaving a tail for sewing up. Thread it through a darning needle and push it through the remaining stitches.

Remove the stitches from the needle. Pull the yarn tightly. Sew up to the cast on edge using mattress stitch, leaving the cast on edges open. Stuff each leg.

TAIL – make one
Cast on 7 stitches in M.
Row 2 P
Rows 3–20 Work in St st
Row 21 K1, SKP, K1, K2tog, K1 (5 sts)
Row 22 P.
Cut the yarn, leaving a tail for sewing up. Thread it through a darning needle and push it through the remaining five stitches. Remove the stitches from the needle. Pull the yarn tightly. Sew up to the cast on edge using mattress stitch, leaving the cast on edges open. Pull the mattress stitch tight to curl the tail.

BUN – make two in B and two in C
Cast on 30 stitches.
Row 2 P all even rows.
Row 3 K
Row 5 K1, Kfb, K to the last 3 stitches, Kfb, K2 (32 sts)
Row 7 K
Row 9 K1, Kfb, K to the last 3 stitches, Kfb, K2 (34 sts)
Row 11 K
Row 13 K2, SKP, K to the last 4 stitches, K2tog, K2 (32 sts)
Row 15 K
Row 17 K2, SKP, K to the last 4 stitches, K2tog, K2 (30 sts)
Row 19 K
Row 21 Cast off loosely.

TOP PIECE – make one
Cast on 5 stitches in M.
Row 2 P all even rows, noting the even row that has been underlined.
Row 3 K1, *Kfb* three times, K1 (8 sts)
Row 5 K
Row 7 K
Row 9 K
Row 11 K
Row 13 K2, Kfb, K1, Kfb, K3 (10 sts)
Row 15 K3, Kfb, K1, Kfb, K4 (12 sts)
Row 16 P [adding colour W markers to the 4th and 9th stitches]
Row 17 K1, Kfb, K2, Kfb, K1, Kfb, K2, Kfb, K2 (16 sts)
Row 19 K [adding a colour X marker to the 6th stitch and a colour Y marker to the 11th stitch]

Row 21 K
Row 23 K [adding a colour X marker to the 6th stitch and a colour Y marker to the 11th stitch]
Row 25 K2, SKP, K1, SKP, K2, K2tog, K1, K2tog, K2 (12 sts)
Row 27 K2, SKP, K4, K2tog, K2 (10 sts)
Row 29 K2, SKP, K2, K2tog, K2 (8 sts)
Row 31 K2, Kfb, K1, Kfb, K3 (10 sts)
Row 33 K2, Kfb, K3 , Kfb, K3 (12 sts)
Rows 35–74 Work from the chart
Here the pattern asks you to work from the chart, which you'll find on page 103. The chart features a yellow line running through it. That's the new colourwork technique. Charts are often used in patterns as they're easier to follow than rows and rows of text.

Row 75 K
Row 77 K
Row 79 K1, SKP, SKP, K2, K2tog, K2tog, K1 (8 sts)
Row 81 K1, SKP, K2, K2tog, K1 (6 sts)
Row 83 Cast off.

SEWING UP
If you get stuck you can find a sewing up video at firsttimeknits.com.

Place a leg in the centre of the four Colour U markers on the under piece. Match the stitches on the first row of the leg to those on the under piece and sew together in M, mimicking a horizontal mattress stitch. On the sides of the legs, where the stitches don't match, sew under and out of the V stitches on the legs and then into the bars between the stitches on the under piece, like a regular mattress stitch. Sew around the leg, leaving the cast on edges open. Place the other leg in the centre of the four colour V markers and sew up. Place the remaining two legs between the sets of colour U and V markers on the other side of the under piece and sew in place. Remove the markers. In between each set of legs add a small stitch in M, about a third of the way up each leg. Sew the legs together to keep them upright. Weave the loose ends into the wrong side.

Place two ear pieces together with the right sides facing up and sew together

from the cast on to the cast off edge using mattress stitch in M. Sew the cast off edges together using horizontal mattress stitch, then sew to the cast on edge using regular mattress stitch. Leave the cast on edges open. Tuck the loose ends into the ear, but don't stuff it. Place the cast on edge of the ear vertically between the colour X markers on the top piece and sew in place using M. Repeat for the second ear, sewing it up and placing it between the colour Y markers. Weave the loose ends into the wrong side. Place the eyes over the colour W markers and secure with washers on the wrong side. Remove all the stitch markers.

Place the top and under pieces together with the right sides facing up. Pin and sew together the cast on edges using horizontal mattress stitch in M. Place the nose in the centre of the cast on seam and secure it with a washer on the wrong side. Pin and sew the cast off edges together using horizontal mattress stitch. Pin one side together, from the cast on to the cast off edge. Sew up using regular mattress stitch in M. Pin the other side together and sew up, leaving a hole. Stuff the body. Sew up the hole and push the darning needle and yarn into the knit of the piece to weave in the loose end, making sure you pull the needle out. Place the tail over the cast off edge seam and sew in place using M. Add a small stitch in M under each ear, into the knit of the head, to keep the ears in place.

Place a B and C bun piece together, with the right sides facing up, and pin together. Sew the sides up using regular mattress stitch in C. Sew the cast on edges together using horizontal mattress stitch and then repeat for the cast off edges, leaving a hole for stuffing. Stuff the bun and sew up the hole. Repeat for the other bun. Place the buns with the C side against the body of the dog and sew in place using C. Mirror the sewing instructions on the other side of the hot dog dog. Push the needle and yarn through the bun to weave in the loose ends.

Stranded colour

You'll never get lost with a chart

My hot dog dog is a great introduction to the vast world of intermediate colour changing. The pattern is worked from a chart, but I have also included the pattern rows. Each square is a stitch and

you read the chart from the bottom to the top. The brown squares are M and the yellow squares are D. As the pattern is written in stocking stitch you follow the chart in the same way – there are

arrows to show this. For clarity, I've used super chunky wool, but you can follow these instructions in the weight you're working in. You can download the chart from firsttimeknits.com.

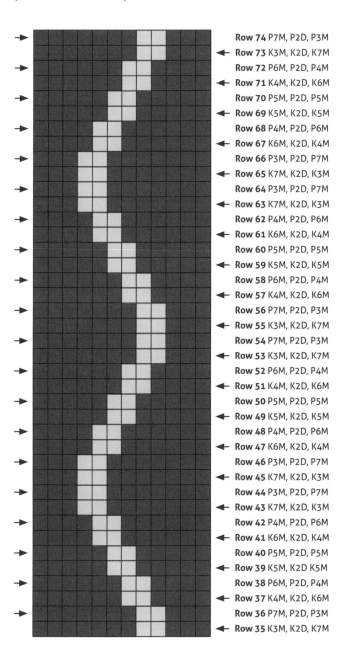

Row 74 P7M, P2D, P3M
Row 73 K3M, K2D, K7M
Row 72 P6M, P2D, P4M
Row 71 K4M, K2D, K6M
Row 70 P5M, P2D, P5M
Row 69 K5M, K2D, K5M
Row 68 P4M, P2D, P6M
Row 67 K6M, K2D, K4M
Row 66 P3M, P2D, P7M
Row 65 K7M, K2D, K3M
Row 64 P3M, P2D, P7M
Row 63 K7M, K2D, K3M
Row 62 P4M, P2D, P6M
Row 61 K6M, K2D, K4M
Row 60 P5M, P2D, P5M
Row 59 K5M, K2D, K5M
Row 58 P6M, P2D, P4M
Row 57 K4M, K2D, K6M
Row 56 P7M, P2D, P3M
Row 55 K3M, K2D, K7M
Row 54 P7M, P2D, P3M
Row 53 K3M, K2D, K7M
Row 52 P6M, P2D, P4M
Row 51 K4M, K2D, K6M
Row 50 P5M, P2D, P5M
Row 49 K5M, K2D, K5M
Row 48 P4M, P2D, P6M
Row 47 K6M, K2D, K4M
Row 46 P3M, P2D, P7M
Row 45 K7M, K2D, K3M
Row 44 P3M, P2D, P7M
Row 43 K7M, K2D, K3M
Row 42 P4M, P2D, P6M
Row 41 K6M, K2D, K4M
Row 40 P5M, P2D, P5M
Row 39 K5M, K2D K5M
Row 38 P6M, P2D, P4M
Row 37 K4M, K2D, K6M
Row 36 P7M, P2D, P3M
Row 35 K3M, K2D, K7M

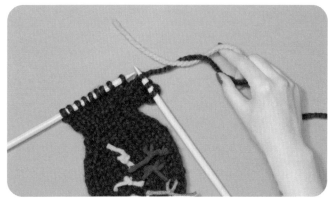

1. The first row of the chart is Row 35 – an odd number so it is a knit row, which you read from right to left. The chart shows three M squares, so knit these in M as usual. Next are two D squares. As you're adding the new D colour in the middle of the row you can't tie it. Instead lay it over the M yarn and twist it. You can tighten up the tail when you weave in later.

Move the M yarn under the D yarn

2. Knit two stitches in D – it's as easy as that! The chart then shows seven squares in M. Move the M yarn under the D yarn and knit the seven stitches. This adds a strand along the back of the work – hence the 'stranded' name. Don't pull the M yarn tightly as it will bunch up the D stitches.

Move the M yarn over the D yarn

3. Turn the piece and start working the next row – this is a purl row so you read the chart from the left to the right. Purl the number of brown squares in M as usual, until you reach the colour change. If you were to start purling in D you'd make a hole in the work. Before changing colour move the D yarn under the M yarn, then purl two stitches in D.

4. After working the stitches in D the chart shows the remaining stitches are knitted in M. As on the knit row, carry the M yarn across the back of the work, but over the D yarn, and purl the stitch as usual. Again, be careful not to pull the strand too much, but at the same time don't leave it too loose. Like with other techniques in knitting, keep it natural.

5. On the next row the colour change moves one stitch to the left. Knit the stitches in M to the colour change. As the M stitch will be over a D stitch you need to prevent a hole from forming. Move the M yarn under the D yarn and knit as usual.

6. You then need to change to the D yarn but, before doing so, move the D yarn under the M yarn and knit the two stitches in D. Then move the M yarn under the D yarn and work the remaining stitches on the chart in M.

7. Follow the chart to Row 46, applying Steps 3–6 to these rows. At Row 47 the chart changes with the D colour change moving to the right. On the odd rows, before knitting the first stitch in D, move the D yarn under the M yarn. Follow the colour changing steps to Row 54.

8. Once you've worked Rows 35–54 the piece will look like this. The stranded yarn technique creates a colour change in the middle of the piece. Work Rows 55–74 from the chart applying these steps. After Row 74, cut the D yarn and weave in the loose ends on the wrong side. Return to the pattern.

Finished projects

How did they get on?

I was really excited to see which yarn my knitters picked for this project. As I said in the first review section, my favourite thing about being a designer is seeing how others make your knits.

I'm secretly hoping someone makes an even bigger hot dog dog than Simon – maybe it'll be you! Each of my knitters picked their weight of yarn and used the needles that the ball band recommended. They followed the same pattern but Zoë and Simon had to adjust the amount of stuffing needed, as well as the eye and nose sizes. See what they used at firsttimeknits.com.

Amala: I used DK yarn and it was a nice change to use the smaller needles. The hot dog dog was so cute, and the yellow sauce was such a cute detail. Because of the weight of yarn I used, it made a lovely toy. If you knitted the hot dog dog in different sizes or types of yarn, you could make a cushion or just a massive hot dog dog!

Katie: I enjoy using chunky needles and yarn but, as this pattern allows you to scale the project up and down, I wanted to try smaller needles. I thought they would be fiddly and it would take ages to make my hot dog dog, but I found I could knit really quickly with them. I'm really proud of how neat my colour change is.

Zoë: I was most excited for this one because I love, love, love little sausage dogs. It looks so cute when finally put together. I think I found it harder to knit on smaller needles, but it was worth it for the little puppy that came out at the end! The colour change was less intense than I thought, and I really enjoyed it.

Simon: I really enjoyed this project. The chart for the stranded colour section was easy to follow, thanks to the directional arrows. Based on this first attempt at the skill I now feel confident trying more complex patterns. The use of chunky yarn was because I prefer the texture of it and it seemed to suit this particular knit.

Project 9:
Raglan jumper
Saving the warmest till last

The last project is a raglan jumper and, like the other knits, you can customize it. You can see lots of design options, including my knitters' versions on page 111 and in the Project 9 section at firsttimeknits.com. If you haven't made the hat from Project 7, I would advise making it first, as the collar of the jumper is also knitted in the round.

SKILL LEVEL INTERMEDIATE

Raglan jumper

MATERIALS

Rico Essentials Big yarn (chunky, 50% wool/50% acrylic , 48m per 50g):

M (main colour)

XS: cropped – 8 balls; cosy – 11 balls
S: cropped – 10 balls; cosy – 13 balls
M: cropped – 11 balls; cosy – 15 balls
L: cropped – 13 balls; cosy – 17 balls
XL: cropped – 15 balls; cosy – 19 balls
XXL: cropped – 18 balls; cosy – 21 balls

A (colour 1)   **B** (colour 2)   **C** (colour 3)
D (colour 4)   **E** (colour 5)
XS, S, M, and L – 1 ball of each colour
XL and XXL – 2 balls of each colour

Stitch holder
Large needles: 8mm (US 11) circular needles
with a 80cm (32in) cable
Small long needles: 6mm (US 10) circular
needles with a 80cm (32in) cable
Small short needles: 6mm (US 10) circular
needles with a 40cm (16in) cable
The jumper is not knitted in the round, but
you'll need to use circular needles. You will
need a pair with a short cable for the collar.

TENSION

11 stitches x 16 rows = 10cm (4in) in St st on 8mm (US 11) needles
Although you're using circular needles, the jumper is not knitted in the round. When using the circular needles use them like two straight needles, but with the cable between them. You're using them because the jumper has too many stitches for a straight pair of needles. Swatch normally, remembering to cast on 4 more stitches and work 4 extra rows.

ABBREVIATIONS

K Knit
Kfb Knit into the front and back of the same stitch (increase)
SKP Slip a stitch, knit a stitch and pass the slipped stitch over (decrease)
St st Stocking stitch: Knit a row, purl a row alternately
K2tog Knit two stitches together (decrease)
... Repeat the instructions within the asterisks
P Purl
(sts) Stitches: The number of stitches you'll have at the end of the row

FINISHED SIZES: UNISEX XS, S, M, L, XL, XXL

Each size is colour coded – follow your colour throughout the pattern. See the size guide with bust and length measurements at firsttimeknits.com. You can also choose to make a 'cropped' jumper or a 'cosy' longer version.

BONUS: If you'd like to work in a different colourway, see page 111 to find out what my knitters decided to do. The Project 9 section at firsttimeknits.com includes these adaptations and other design options.

Use the long tail cast on – this creates the first row of knitting. Each part of this pattern will begin from Row 2.

BACK – make one
Using the small long needles, cast on 52, 58, 64, 70, 76, 82 stitches in A.
RIB
Row 2 *K1, P1* all stitches
Row 3 Change to B, *K1, P1* all stitches
Row 4 *K1, P1* all stitches
Row 5 Change to C, *K1, P1* all stitches
Row 6 *K1, P1* all stitches
Row 7 Change to D, *K1, P1* all stitches
Row 8 *K1, P1* all stitches
Row 9 Change to E, *K1, P1* all stitches
Row 10 *K1, P1* all stitches
There are two length options (cropped and cosy). Follow your design's pattern.

CROPPED JUMPER
Rows 11–36 Change to the large needles and M, working all stitches in it from here on. Work in St st.

COSY JUMPER
Rows 11–66 Change to the large needles and M, working all stitches in it from here on. Work in St st.

ARM SHAPING
Reset the row counter to 0.
Here you're asked to reset the row counter back to 0. You don't need to cast off and start a new piece – just keep working the piece but with the row count set back to 0.
Row 1 Cast off 4, 4, 6, 6, 6, 8 stitches at the beginning of the row. K to the end of the row (48, 54, 58, 64, 70, 74 sts)
Row 2 Cast off 4, 4, 6, 6, 6, 8 stitches purlwise at the beginning of the row. P to the end of the row (44, 50, 52, 58, 64, 66 sts)
To cast off purlwise, purl two stitches. Then, like casting off knitwise, transfer the first stitch over and off the needle.
Row 3 K
Row 4 P

Row 5 K2, SKP, K to the last four stitches, K2tog, K2 (42, 48, 50, 56, 62, 64 sts)
Row 6 P
Here the pattern splits for the different sizes. Follow your chosen size, then move to the decreasing section.
XS and S repeat **Rows 3–6** two more times (38, 44 sts)
M and L repeat **Rows 3–6** three more times (44, 50 sts)
XL repeat **Rows 3–6** five more times (52 sts)
XXL repeat **Rows 3–6** six more times (52 sts)

DECREASING – ALL SIZES
Here the split ends and all the sizes follow the same pattern.
Reset the row counter to 0.
Row 1 K2, SKP, K to the last four stitches, K2tog, K2 (36, 42, 42, 48, 50, 50 sts)
Row 2 P
Repeat **Rows 1 and 2** until you have 20, 20, 22, 24, 26, 28 sts remaining.

The repeat finishes with Row 2 so, after achieving the right stitch count, make sure you purl.
Next Row: Cast off loosely.

FRONT
Using the small long needles, cast on 52, 58, 64, 70, 76, 82 stitches in A. Work from the **BACK** pattern until you have 30, 30, 32, 34, 36, 38 stitches. Make sure to work the purl row after achieving the right stitch count.
Often garment patterns will ask you to repeat the back piece until a certain point. Work the rib, the St st, the arm shaping and the decreasing until you have the required number of stitches.

NECK SHAPING
Reset the row counter to 0.
Row 1 K2, SKP, K7, tie a new ball of yarn to the yarn you're knitting with and use it to cast off 8, 8, 10, 12, 14, 16 stitches in the centre of the work. On the side before the cast off, don't cut the yarn. Slide the 10 stitches onto a stitch holder – these will be the left front. **Stitch holders are big safety pins and will keep the stitches safe.**
On the side after the centre cast off, K6 (you'll have 7 stitches on the right needle including the last stitch cast off over), K2tog, K2. You'll have 10 stitches.
Row 2 P
Row 3 Cast off 1 stitch at the start of the row, K4 (there will be 5 stitches on the right needle), K2tog, K2 (8 sts)
Row 4 P
Row 5 Cast off 1 stitch at the start of the row, K2 (there will be 3 stitches on the right needle), K2tog, K2 (6 sts)
Row 6 P
Row 7 Cast off 1 stitch, K2tog, K2 (4 sts)
Row 8 P
Row 9 Cast off 1 stitch, K2tog (2 sts)
Row 10 P
Row 11 Cast off as usual.

LEFT NECK – RIGHT HAND SIDE
Slide the stitches on the stitch holder onto the left-hand needle ready to be worked from Row 2 (a purl row). **Make sure you don't twist the stitches while doing so (see page 72).**
Row 2 Using the yarn you left behind, cast off 1 stitch purlwise, P8 (9 sts)

Row 3 K2, SKP, K5 (8 sts)
Row 4 Cast off 1 stitch purlwise at the start of the row, P6 (7 sts)
Row 5 K2, SKP, K3 (6 sts)
Row 6 Cast off 1 stitch purlwise at the start of the row, P4 (5 sts)
Row 7 K2, SKP, K1 (4 sts)
Row 8 Cast off 1 stitch purlwise at the start of the row, P2 (3 sts)
Row 9 SKP, K1 (2 sts)
Row 10 P
Row 11 Cast off as usual.

SLEEVES – make two
Using the small long needles, cast on 24, 26, 30, 30, 30, 30 stitches in A. Work Rows 2–10 of the **RIB** from the **BACK** pattern, then return to here.
Row 11 Change to the larger needles and M, working all stitches in it from here on. Work in St st. K1, Kfb, K to the last 2 stitches, Kfb, K1 (26, 28, 32, 32, 32, 32 sts)
Row 12 P
Here the pattern splits. Follow your size, then follow ALL SIZES.
XS, S, M
Reset the row counter to 0.
Row 1 K
Row 2 P
Row 3 K
Row 4 P
Row 5 K
Row 6 P
Row 7 K1, Kfb, K to the last 2 stitches, Kfb, K1 (28, 30, 34 sts)
Row 8 P
Repeat Rows 1–8 two more times (32, 34, 38 sts)
Then follow the instructions below.
XS, S, M, L
Reset the row counter to 0.
Row 1 K
Row 2 P
Row 3 K
Row 4 P
Row 5 K1, Kfb, K to the last 2 stitches, Kfb, K1 (34, 36, 40, 34 sts)
Row 6 P
For XS repeat **Rows 1–6** once (36 sts). Then work 18 rows in St st.
For S and M repeat **Rows 1–6** three more times (42, 46 sts). Then work 6 rows in St st.
For L repeat **Rows 1–6** eight more times (50 sts)

XL, XXL
Row 1 K
Row 2 P
Row 3 K1, Kfb, K to the last 2 stitches, Kfb, K1 (34, 34 sts)
Row 4 P
Repeat **Rows 1–4** seven times (48, 48 sts)
Reset the row counter to 0.
Row 1 K
Row 2 P
Row 3 K
Row 4 P
Row 5 K1, Kfb, K to the last 2 stitches, Kfb, K1 (50, 50 sts)
Row 6 P
Repeat **Rows 1–6** two more times (54, 54 sts). Then work 4 rows in St st.

ALL SIZES – ARM SHAPING
Apply the arm shaping and decreases from the back piece until you have 6 stitches, finishing with a purl row. **These raglan jumpers use the same decreases on the sleeves as they do on the back and front. The stitch count will be different but the formula is the same. Download the tick sheet for the sleeves (which includes the stitch count) from firsttimeknits.com.**
After working the decreases, reset the row counter to 0.
Row 1 K1, SKP, K2tog, K1 (4 sts)
Row 2 P
Row 3 Cast off loosely.

SEWING UP
Head to page 109 for the sewing up tutorial. You need to sew up before adding the collar.

COLLAR
Following on from Step 10 on page 110, work Rows 2–10 of the **RIB** pattern from the **BACK**. Then return to here.
Rows 11–20 Work in **RIB**, reversing the colour order from the **BACK** pattern, starting with E and ending with A. Cast off loosely in A. Fold the rib in half – the cast off edge will sit against the picked up stitches. As the collar is knitted in rib, thread the loose tails into the wrong side of the rib. Weave each tail in following the same method of weaving into an inside seam. You can see my video tutorial at firsttimeknits.com.

Sewing up and neckline

Finishing your jumper

You've knitted all the pieces and you're ready to sew up your jumper. It's nice to take a little extra care when sewing up garments as you'll be wearing them, after all! You can follow these steps or watch me sew one in the Project 9 section at firsttimeknits.com. I'm demonstrating on a cropped version of the rainbow rib jumper, but you can apply these steps to the cosy version as all that's different is the length under the decrease section. After sewing up, you'll be picking up the neckline using the small short circular needles and then knitting the collar onto it.

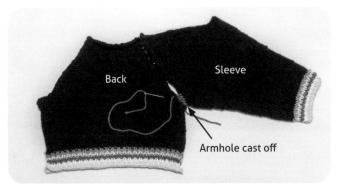

1. Lay the back piece of the jumper flat with the right side facing up. Lay a sleeve, with the right side facing up, next to the back so that the decrease sections meet. Pin in place from the cast off armholes to the neckline. Then sew the cast off sections of the armholes together using horizontal mattress stitch. I'm using a contrast colour to demonstrate.

2. Pull the yarn tightly to secure the armhole cast off pieces together. Tuck the loose ends behind the jumper – you'll weave them in later. Then, using the same piece of yarn, sew up to the neck using regular mattress stitch. As with the hot dog dog, you can sew two bars at a time. Once you've reached the neck, weave the loose ends into the inside seam.

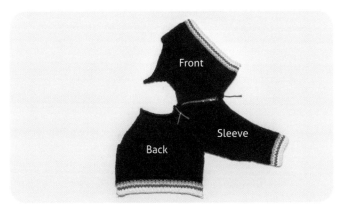

3. Once the sleeve has been sewn on, place the front piece against it so the decrease sections of the front and the sleeve match. Sew the pieces together following Steps 1 and 2. Sew the other sleeve to the front and back piece, following the instructions from Steps 1 and 2. All the decrease sections of the pieces will be sewn together.

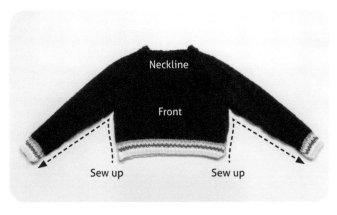

4. Lay the jumper so that the cast on edges of the body meet. Sew the left side up from the rib, making sure that all the stripes match, using the A yarn. Start with a figure of eight and sew up using regular mattress stitch – it will still work on the rib. Switch to M and sew up the body all the way to the sleeve's rib. Sew up the rib using A. Repeat for the other side.

5. For the collar of jumper you need to pick up the stitches along the cast off neckline. You'll need the smaller shorter cable needles. Place the jumper so that the back is facing you with the right side facing up. Push one of the needles through middle of the V of the first stitch after the sewing seam on the right-hand side. Take the A yarn and loop it around the tip of the needle, leaving a tail.

6. Hold the A yarn from the ball and the tail tightly. Using your left index finger, push the needle tip down and out of the stitch. This will catch the yarn looped around it and create a stitch on the needle. You've just picked up a stitch! Pick up every stitch across the back piece of the work until you reach the seam on the other side. There are 18, 18, 20, 22, 24, 26 stitches in total to pick up.

7. Once you've picked up the stitches across the back piece of the neck, you'll come to the top of the sleeves. There are two stitches to pick up here. They can be harder to see because they're at the top of the decrease stitches at the top of the sleeve. You'll need to pick those up too. Your stitch count will be 20, 20, 22, 24, 26, 28.

8. Turn the jumper so the front is facing you. Pull the needle so the stitches move along the cable to the other needle. This will free up the working needle to move around. Find the first stitch on the front and pick it up, then pick up the stitches across the neckline. Work into the four stitches that have been cast off over. You will pick up five stitches in total.

9. You now need to pick up the stitches in the centre cast off section of the neckline. There will be a gap between the last stitch picked up to the first one on the cast off. Don't worry about the gap – just pick it up. Pick up the 9, 9, 11, 13, 15, 17 stitches across the centre cast off. Then pick up the five stitches on the other side of the neckline. Again, look for the ones under the bar of the cast off stitch above them.

10. Pick up the last two stitches on the other sleeve – there'll be 41, 41, 45, 49, 53, 57 in total. This counts as the first row. Add a stitch marker to the right needle. Work in the round from here. The second row is *K1, P1* but, as there's an odd number of stitches, K2tog the first two stitches and pull them tightly, reducing the stitch count by one. P the next stitch, then continue to work *K1, P1* rib. Return to the pattern.

Finished projects

How did they get on?

This is it! I've run out of pages and it's time to say goodbye. It's been an amazing journey, watching my knitters grow from garter stitch caterpillars to butterflies in raglan jumpers. I'd love to know how you got on and to see your finished projects too. The raglan jumper is a big project so, when I saw my knitters, we chatted away over tea and supermarket snacks. At one point they all agreed it was similar to making a big hat, with the rib stitch, stocking stitch and the decreasing. So, without further ado, here are my knitters in their finished knitted jumpers.

Amala: I really liked making the jumper. It's important to pay attention to the increases and decreases so that everything fits together. Make sure that you add a new ball of yarn at the end of a row, so you don't get bumps in the middle of it. It was so nice to have something lovely and warm to wear at the end of it.

Katie: I chose the colours for my jumper as they're some of my favourites and they go with most of my wardrobe. After feeling confident with knit and purl this was quicker to knit than I expected. It was challenging sewing it up neatly and picking up the neckline. If I was to knit it again I'd choose the smaller size to fit me better.

Simon: I strongly believe in using the resources we already have, so I chose to use the leftover yarn from the other jumpers. I also love colourful clothing and asymmetrical design. I struggled with knowing if I'd picked up enough stitches for the neckline and I used DPNs as I preferred them to the circular needles.

Zoë: I love cropped jumpers because I'm always wearing high-waisted trousers, so it's the perfect length. I wanted to combine two colours that felt very wintery. Because I used chunky yarn I felt like the jumper developed really quickly. It was difficult to get the right tension, so I had to experiment with different needles before I got it right.

About the author

It's me, Louise! I've been chatting away to you throughout this book. I'm an award-winning knitting pattern designer with a degree in commercial photography. I live in Sheffield, UK, and run Sincerely Louise from the top floor of an old cutlery factory. I spend my days designing patterns, making kits and running my business. Most nights you'll find me knitting and watching Coronation Street. I love going to gigs at DIY music venues, chippy teas, Dalmatian print, gargoyles and Silver Apples.

Acknowledgements

This book is dedicated to Peter Butler, who has spent countless hours working on the design, helped with photography and listened to me talk about knitting for, well, since we first met. Not only has he supported me through the process of writing *First Time Knits*, but throughout my whole crafty journey and he's truly amazing.

I'd like to thank my four knitters for taking part in what has been the most exciting chapter in my career. Meeting them and seeing how quickly they learnt to knit has been an unforgettable experience. I'm grateful for Amala's critical eye, Katie's incredible positivity, Simon's enthusiasm for craft and Zoe's passion for life. I'd also like to thank Katie, Bella, Michelle, Alice and the Pavilion team for the opportunity to write this book, their support while making it, to Jeni the copy editor and to Marilyn, a fantastic pattern checker.

Suppliers

Sincerely Louise
Wool, kits, accessories and mounting boards
www.sincerelylouise.co.uk
www.firsttimeknits.com

Plymouth Yarn
www.plymouthyarn.com

Patons
www.knitpatons.com

Scheepjes
www.scheepjes.com

Stylecraft
www.stylecraft-yarns.co.uk

Rico
www.rico-design.de

Techniques index

Also by this author